Spiritual Insights
for Daily Living

TRIGUEIRINHO

Spiritual Insights for Daily Living: Selections from the Work of José Trigueirinho Netto

Shasti Association

Copyright 2022 Shasti Association

The profits generated from sales of books by Trigueirinho and his associates will be used to support the non-profit activities of the Shasti Association to disseminate their work

Translated and edited by Alan David Berkowitz (Micha-El) and Magda Beatriz Rockett Berkowitz (Gran)

Cataloging-in-Publication Data

Trigueirinho Netto, José

Spiritual Insights for Daily Living: Selections from the Work of José Trigueirinho Netto Trigueirinho.

Mount Shasta, CA, Shasti Association, 1st edition, 2022 177 p.

ISBN: 978-1-948430-15-9
Library of Congress Control Number: 2022944244

1. Body-Mind-Spirit
2. New Age
3. Occult Science

I. Title.

English language rights reserved
P.O. Box 318
Mt. Shasta, CA 96067-0318
editorial@shasti.org
www.shasti.org

Contents

To Fulfill the Supreme Will	1
Lack of Control in Civilization Today	4
Attitudes That Are No Longer Adequate	6
Global Warming	8
The Contemplative Life	10
How to Control Thoughts	13
The Force of the Being is What Can Transform the World	16
The Key to Illumination	19
The Great Cosmic Voyage	21
Opening Oneself to Planetary Consciousness	23
The Energy of Power	25
Mercy	27
Impassiveness	29
Impersonality	31
The Awakening of a New Consciousness	34
Aggressions Committed by Humanity of the Surface	36
Karmic Accounts	38
Family	40
The Law of Detachment	42
Superior Knowledge	44
The Way to the Path of Healing	46
Fundamental Activities with Money	49
The Mind and Evolutionary Work	51

The Inner Key	53
The Art of Weaving	55
The Quietude that Contains All the Answers	58
To Reach the Goal	62
The Tests and the Heir	65
Departures with Joy	67
Times of Reunion	70
After Transforming Yourself, Help and Teach Others	72
Diseases	75
Faith	77
The Keys to Cross the Sacred Portal	80
Understanding the Correct Use of Money	83
After the Darkness	85
Listen Pilgrim	87
Empty Yourself	90
The Role of Those Who Know the True Situation of Planet Earth	92
The Relationship of Humanity with Money	94
To Withdraw the Senses – This is What You Have to Do	98
Three Kinds of Actions	101
The Student and Prayer	103
To Know How to Be Free	106
The Pilgrim and the Serious Man	108
A New Universe	110
The Miracle	112
Humanity Today	114

Extreme Times	117
The Law of Purification	119
The Feminine Polarity	121
For Those Who Have Decided to Serve the Planet	123
True Prayer	125
To Divinize Matter	128
Where to Place Thought and Aspiration To Learn to See	130
	132
Inevitable Conflicts	134
Falling Asleep Correctly	136
Awakening Correctly	139
Involutionary Forces	142
Letting Yourself Be Led by Wisdom A Crucial Moment	144
	146
About Trigueirinho and His Work	150
Books by Trigueirinho	154
Audios of Trigueirinho	165

To Fulfill the Supreme Will

One day, a man dressed as a peasant started walking around his land. He was deeply loved by everyone and had devoted his whole life to managing the area, always trying to do the best for the well-being of all. For five moons he traveled secretly through villages and towns until he was recognized by three of his subjects. The first one asked him:

"Master, I bow before you and ask you, what can I do to better serve your noble purposes and to deserve your reward?"

The second one asked him:

"Master, you who are so powerful, what else can you do to help us?" And the third said:

"I fulfill your orders, Master, just as I obey the Life that speaks to me in different forms at each moment. At sunrise and in the darkness of the night, in the heat of summer and in the coldness of winter, in the heat of work in the field and in the refreshing waters of the waterfall, a silent and hidden Voice is always speaking. In reality and in humility I tell you: I serve the One Lord, the one who created the universe and the stars, the sun, the moon and the planets, who created the water, earth and all other elements; to Him I dedicate total obedience."

Hearing these words, the Master of the land recognized this servant as his heir, thus showing that the purpose of his trip was fulfilled. Then he said to the young man:

"Follow me, because I also dedicate my life and my existence to the One Lord. We are brothers and companions on the same journey. Follow me, because from now on you will have this land to rule. Are you ready to follow me?"

The young man answered:

"I do not search for earthly power, master. Neither for possessions or material goods. I only try to fulfill the Will of that One who outlines the destiny of the cosmos."

The master concluded:

Then you are ready. Follow me.

"Travel Through Subtle Worlds" 63-64

Lack of Control in Civilization Today

The degradation of today's civilization, which is also reflected in diseases like AIDS, is deplorable. When human beings repeatedly devote themselves to their own satisfaction, the capacity to surpass the conditions that are exterminating their life is lost. Then one is left with the harm, without the means to overcome it.

On the concrete level, few, very few, are free from the effects of the material degradation of this humanity. Besides, most are not turned to that which, within themselves, is immortal and unharmed by the game of the degenerative forces. Nonetheless, this whole play is being led to its conclusion by a superior power.

For those with little experience, it could be alarming to notice humanity's suffering as, for example, the pain which results from sexual promiscuity, which today is considered natural. Due to this lack of control, certain diseases proliferate, causing irreparable damage. Some, although not considered severe, affect genetic features and perpetuate themselves for generations. Moreover, under normal conditions, it would require from three to seven consecutive incarnations with patterns of a high degree of purity for them to be removed from an individual, something not easy to bring about in the present civilization.

The elimination of these degenerative forces, impregnated in the aura of an individual, is possible by means of supra-physical implantation of a new genetic code,* but -- depending on the extent to which they have infiltrated, the destruction of ancient permanent atoms of the material bodies and the formation of new ones may be necessary.

*New genetic code. A new genetic code is being implanted in the inner levels of those beings who respond to spiritual stimuli. This code, the GNA, is constituted by genes originating from incorporeal planets, free from aggressiveness and violence.

"New Oracles" pp. 63-64

Attitudes That Are No Longer Adequate

In the planetary kingdom, which includes many worlds, there are also imperfect worlds with races on the surface that still live under the law of birth and death. When these worlds have not achieved the knowledge of the perfect law, they will retain aggressive attitudes as happens among the humans on the surface of Earth. Having developed technology for the purpose of subordinating others, humans now try to conquer the cosmos. This is impossible because, like everyone else, humanity lives within the limits that correspond to the degree of evolution that they have achieved.

You have been informed that on several occasions explosions were heard and rains of fire were seen in the atmosphere or in the skies of this planet. What has happened is that spaceships that are working in the orbit of the Earth have accomplished the "involution" of other spaceships that intended to invade the planet and take advantage of it. There are extraterrestrial civilizations (less evolved cosmic races) that would occupy earth in order to maintain it under the influence of the evil forces that still direct it. They would do this to impede the transformation of Earth, but this transformation is already under way and follows the evolutionary plan.

The explosions mentioned occurred in the south of Argentina, in Buenos Aires and in Mendoza, and were produced as a result of the custodial spaceships that, in the thousands, are taking care of Earth's security.

You do not need to fear from here onwards, because a perfect work is being done in this way until the time when humanity of the surface, through its new race, will be included in the Interplanetary and Intergalactic Councils and consequently, will have the necessary access to many facts currently unknown. As the laws of the other planes become known, in turn more knowledge of these facts will reoccur. This will come with time and this time is approaching rapidly.

"Miz Tli Tlan, An Awakening World" pp. 176-177

Global Warming

Q. At this moment we are following the statements made by scientists of the whole world about global warming and its consequences for the planet. What do you think, Sir, about this topic?

A. Global warming is one among many serious dangers that menace the planet and humanity. The prospect of great planetary disasters is being presented timidly and in an attenuated way by science and by communication media. We know that the real planetary situation is not openly revealed in part not to disturb the business world, to not affect tourism, and for many other reasons. However, although most of the information has been provided discretely, today there is no one who does not have an idea of what awaits us. There are facts that appear catastrophic but that in reality contain transformative revelations as, for example, what is about to happen in Antarctica.

Q. What can we still do? Can the catastrophes be avoided?

A. Well, the most important thing is prayer. Pray and contribute as little as possible to the aggravating of the general situation. I must clarify that by praying, I want to say to search for more elevated and profound levels of consciousness, where there is harmony, peace and the balancing of our being. The center of our soul is the only secure place. It is a place within us that negative and destructive forces cannot reach. At this point it is not only planetary catastrophes which have become irreversible. The psychic balance in general is becoming more and more fragile. Discernment and knowledge has become distant from the common life of the majority of people. The reason to live has been lost. We have to position ourselves in a decisive and firm way in our inner self and so be able to help those who are in difficulty -- and as you can see, a great part of the population is already in a precarious condition.

"Signs of Figueira" – Questions to Trigueirinho.
Number 16, 2nd semester 2008

The Contemplative Life

There was a King from a faraway land who once decided to descend from the high towers of his palace, passing through the narrow paths that led to the valleys and further on to the frontiers and then, as if he were a common man, he joined himself to the common people who lived there.

He never said anything about his origin and demanded nothing for his subsistence. He lived a simple life as did the other people, and being a living example of the rectitude of laws and inner principles and even when within his being arose the memories of his real Home he, who had chosen to serve, praised the opportunity to be in the valleys, without the magnificence and the royal ornaments.

Still not yet being aware of who they were receiving, his new companions barely perceived what he was silently radiating. There was a day however, when the messengers of the Kingdom, having left in search of His Majesty, arrived at these lost lands. The luminous procession curved itself before the one who lived as a beggar! In a chariot of fire, he was raised to the level of his Home, higher than rays of Light, leaving the marks of his passage engraved in the heart of humans.

***

The energy that permeates these devotional instructions brings, impressed within itself, the vibration of the immaterial sphere of consciousness. Their projection into the material strata is representative of the new state of realization of the planet Earth and is an indication of the times that are approaching. The presence of individuals in Monasteries must be one of the bridges between two worlds; its religious life can be the base that gives stability to this connection; their unconditional surrender to the Creator, the master key to all tests. Only through surrender can we rise up the steps of a staircase that does not have beginning nor end and which can only be recognized in the inner silence.

In the manifestation of the monastic consciousness there is no half-way; so if a hermetic life has to be assumed externally, it must be even more in perfect wholeness inwardly.

It is in the true love for the Creator that the correct love for all creatures can be lived.

"From Struggle to Peace" pp. 145, 146, 147 and 149

How to Control Thoughts

Thinking is an activity that, for most of humanity, fixes the mind on concrete, external and visible things.

For a person who has still not learned that the thoughts can be controlled they will become wild. And the more they become out of control, the more the mind fixes itself on external and concrete things, and, more difficult it becomes for it to concentrate itself on abstract and elevated things. So, the mind distracts itself, disperses itself, and focuses itself on that which the senses present. And many times the person is not even aware of their own dispersion.

Whoever is conscious of their own state of dispersion and is on a spiritual search wants to concentrate themselves, because only in this way can they centralize the mental energy and direct it to more elevated levels of existence.

However, in order to concentrate oneself it is simply not enough to want to do so, nor to also do disciplined exercises. Concentration only in fact occurs when the person gives up whatever attracts, pleases and makes them happy and turns themselves primarily to the spiritual search.

In the past were created many concentration exercises that were appropriate for the mind of those times. But, in general, those who did the exercises had an organized, harmonious, healthy and disciplined life.

This is not the case for most people today. At present, our civilization stimulates consumerism and a form of disorganized life, led by desires. Somebody who today does the concentration exercises created in the past while living as most people do presently, giving in to the appeals of desires, will not be able to concentrate because they will be lacking a certain asceticism in daily life that is indispensable for concentration.

Moreover, with the passing of time, the consciousness and the human mind developed itself and the mind approximated itself to various levels of consciousness. Therefore, ancient concentration exercises are no longer adequate for the present mind.

When one practices asceticism, that is, when one gives up everything that distracts, when one repels everything that does not lead to spiritual levels, when one controls one's own day by day impulses, then concentration can finally take place.

"Spiritual Work with the Mind" pp. 19-21.

The Force of the Being is What Can Transform the World

Great is the necessity for people to become conscious of the inner life. The awakening to that which each individual keeps within is pressing, because it is not the strength of words that can transform the world, but the force of the being. The power of transformation is more what the being is, in essence, than that which the being does externally.

In general, the situation of the terrestrial being is so lacking in Light that if Light is given to someone, they will refuse it. However, the aspiration towards spiritual levels must be greater than the desire for the world so we can receive the Food that provides us with the conditions to live in Eternity. This Food, that does not arrive unless we search for it, is only given to us in the amount we need.

Sooner or later, we will all be placed before the doorway of surrender. One day we will arrive at a state which does not have books to instruct us, hands to sustain us, words to answer our demands: nothing that will satisfy us. Then it will be time to find the "only reason," and to place our life in it.

When seeing people moving unconsciously like blind ones, what do you think of doing? Realize in yourself whatever you need to achieve perfection in fulfilling the law, so that this perfection can come closer to your brothers and sisters.

You can do nothing for them, but must only fulfill what is yours to do. There is no other path to walk than that which is yours. And know that if you assume it in its entirety you will lighten every else's path. When you deviate from your goal to see what you would do in your brother or sister's place, you put the clarity of your own path in danger.

The destiny of each individual is for them and for the Absolute to plan. How could you interfere in this communion? Even if this Great Consciousness expresses Itself to someone else through you, it is not you who are doing it. So remove from your eyes the blindfold of human compassion and wash them in the pure source of Divine Wisdom. You have lost infinite opportunities to grow in spiritual compassion under the pretext of being tied to inferior planes due to someone or to some situation. Only by being what you are in Spirit, can you be there for your brothers and sisters.

"Time for Healing (The Occult Life)" pp. 70-71.

The Key to Illumination

The key to the illumination of humanity is in the relationship among the three levels (i.e. form, consciousness and essence) of manifestation of life in each cycle. However to be granted the knowledge and the power to express the law, it is not sufficient to have knowledge of the existence of these three levels, because this power and knowledge is derived from contacting a nucleus within oneself that is beyond this triple manifestation and its root.

There is a principle that unites the material particles and the intangible life. This principle which allows the co-existence of the worlds must be found by the human being so that by knowing it, one can collaborate intelligently in the great work of Creation. It is therefore important that an inextinguishable fervor moves the being to search for it. Each overcoming prepares us to live through more subtle tests.

The pain of being immersed in ignorance has to reach unbearable limits so that we will forget everything that concerns ourselves and transform ourselves into a channel for the liberation of others. Having reached higher levels we will, on uncountable occasions, have to help those who are imprisoned in forms, deluded by the fleeting movements.

One who really serves the evolutionary purpose deepens their energy in the sublimity of the cosmos, in intelligence and in matter, placing a focus on the harmony of the three worlds. In this work the tuning of consciousness must be accompanied in a special way, by the strengthening and the elevating of the vibration of the bodies. It is especially necessary to act dispassionately without involvement in that which occurs in the concrete levels. It is also necessary to learn the spontaneity of Nature in which death, life, and transformation are common facts.

"New Oracles" - pp. 106-107.

The Great Cosmic Voyage

Everything that was created throughout time and that around which humanity gravitates will be dissolved. Crowds ran after chimeras and fought for them as if they had consistency, chimeras that by a strong wind will be reduced to nothing. Just as an ephemeral peace is felt when desires are fulfilled, so the forces of illusion have made most people believe that in order to find the ultimate peace all desires would have to be satisfied. The pure beauty and order of divine expressions came to be understood as luxury and comfort. Great mistakes... in which the superfluous installs itself and truth and illusion become mixed up.

Aware of these principles, each human being should prepare themselves for a great cosmic voyage. Vibrations that are attuned with the destiny that awaits us in our minds should prevail. Any desire that is welcomed steals the energy that should be dedicated to this preparation, deviating it to dreaming and from a means to realize it. It is necessary to know that there is a liberating power that cauterizes wounds from thousands of mistakes: it is an attribute of divine energy present in the heart of the being's essence.

"New Oracles"pp. 68

Opening Oneself to Planetary Consciousness

When the disciple recognizes that an incarnated life is only a brief second of the total existence, then that which they intend to achieve as an external realization is re-evaluated. And a wide universe without restrictive parameters silently reveals itself.

It is very important that in these phases we do not place obstacles to the sacred process that the spirit tries to implement through the intermediary of our bodies. It is rare to be able to merge in oneself form and non-form in a way that is beyond the states of diversity and to penetrate unity, where classifications do not exist.

Those who are tuned into this process must find a new axis of alignment and permit their own consciousness to transcend the already known planes.

In the case of those who have already surpassed individual aspects and who let themselves be absorbed in the group consciousness, the next step to take is to open themselves in a hidden and silent way, to the planetary consciousness, living integrated with the energies that sustain the life of the kingdoms, peoples and elements that evolve on Earth. This is the path to know the radiation of the coming times and to allow oneself to be permeated by it. This is also the path to interact with the Hierarchy in a fluid and continuous way.

Imbuing oneself with the stimulus that moves consciousnesses to planetary service and uniting oneself with the objective of the Hierarchy is to get nearer to its tasks and to the ability to not overlook the pain of those who are crushed by the violence of the material forces of this civilization. If there is a way to help dissolve this evil it should be fully assumed and concretized. It is necessary for the individual to reach a certain degree of inner freedom in order to serve in this way. As long as we are in hands of the forces that devastate human life, we will not be able to be an instrument for redemption.

"New Oracles" pp. 45-46

The Energy of Power

Whenever a group of beings is gathered around ideals, evolutionary or not, there is created a concentration of forces that little by little, assumes the characteristics of an entity in the subtle levels. Depending on the quality of the vibration of these ideals, this entity stimulates positive or negative actions in the beings with which it is linked.

The imperialist ideals allied with the distorted use of the energy of power, which lead to vindictive and conquering patriotic feelings that have been cultivated for decades were produced in the beginning of this century and generated entities that held influence over the masses in such a way that it was possible to revive subconscious remains and to fuel war. The discord among great powers created an open field for the action of the forces engendered by them.

In reality, the cruelty and violence that was manifested in the world wars already existed among humans. The negative entities that they represented already lived in the psychic sub-worlds of the planet. A breaking out of conflict can be seen as the recognition of an infection caused by an evil agent: even if there is a great suffering, it has to be eliminated. The relationship among the nations realized itself across time always with objectives of exploitation. The absence of an opening to positive relationships, of mutual and sincere help, brought about conflicts throughout the centuries that were often unconscious, able to be triggered when hidden areas of the human consciousness receive certain stimuli.

"A New Astrological Impulse" pp. 119

Mercy

A divine energy which could be called mercy, raises the human being to levels that are unattainable within the normal processes of the law of karma. This powerful and wise energy flows through impersonal prayer and imparts healing, harmony and liberation.

Despite the fact that, throughout the ages, the word mercy has taken on a strong emotional charge, in its purest sense it denotes this energy that heals and transforms on material, human and psychological levels. Through divine mercy, positive karmic residues that remained 'on file' can change situations and bring about circumstances that are more favorable for the development of consciousness.

This mercy is the response given by the inner world to a need felt by individuals, by all humanity or by the planet. For example, divine mercy is manifested when someone has done everything possible to advance along the path to liberation but cannot overcome the limitation of the material bodies. This energy comes from spiritual levels and is the basis for forgiveness. It characterizes the continual help offered to humankind by the Hierarchies* even though humans seldom respond to these incentives.

The principal misunderstanding of those who transgress the law is to consider that their error is greater than divine mercy; because of this, they do not allow themselves to receive it.

*Hierarchies. Consciousnesses that have transcended the material laws and have ascended the sublime steps of spiritual existence. As a unified and cohesive body, they transmit directives for the fulfillment of the evolutionary purpose to the inhabitants of the universe where they work.

"Beyond Karma" Irdin Editora , pp. 54-55
(English edition)

Impassiveness

At the same time as the contact with one's own Monad and with the Hierarchies deepens itself to greater consciousness, the necessity becomes pressing for the individual to surpass certain limits imposed by the normal rhythm of functioning of the terrestrial bodies and to finally live in the three dimensional world as the Son of the Cosmos, the bearer of the Flame and of the Light of the stars.

The ability to be completely impassive before anything that is in this phase is something that is not only desirable, but is a requirement. Without the quality of impassiveness incorporated and lived in the trials of the material world, the being cannot cross the boundary of human consciousness and, in a definitive way, enter into the sublime portals of Cosmic Knowledge.

Only when the energies of our bodies are totally elevated, sublimated and liberated can one can reach this state, one where nothing can disturb us. But the process that we use to reach it must be spontaneous, without thought and conducted internally by the Hierarchies in charge of collaborating with our Monad, be it in the creation of a new civilization or in transmigrating ourselves to other points or planes of the Cosmos.

"Mirna Jad – Inner Sanctuary" p. 139

Impersonality

Many facts of the interior world are revealed to humans as their consciousness becomes permeated by impersonality.

Impersonality begins to emerge through a contact with the higher self, but it expresses itself fully only when the monadic energies start flowing freely through the bodies. Therefore one cannot reach impersonality by means of human effort: it is the fruit of an individual's surrender to the Regent*, to that which is most elevated in the inner being of one's self. However, one can prepare the path to receive this precious seed that reaches material life from the sublime worlds. This preparation is done by detachment from what is known, by renouncing the tendencies of the ego, and by searching for the unique essence of life present in everything and in everybody.

It is not through dealing indifferently with others that impersonality is manifested in the external planes. On the contrary, those who know the Truth bow themselves with reverence to all beings and to them offer the exact portion of energy that is needed, leading the others by means of their surrender and their radiation to release their earthly ties and to contact wider horizons.

In order to see the sunrise, you have to climb high mountains. Only there, far away from the scenery of personal life, can you bathe yourself in the rays of the true existence which daily invite us to be reborn.

Do not try to do with your hands that which the Spirit must do in you. Let yourself transform into a pure flame of devotion and elevate yourself to the Creator. In this way, and only in this way, will you be able to see His sublime face reflected in all your brothers and sisters and together with them, fulfill the task that was assigned to you.

A new reality can already be seen in the planet, the reality of the Spirit that, free from the material chains, elevates Earth to heaven, bringing from there the sacred balms of coming times. You are part of this great Work, you are bearers of the new seed.

Water it then with the pure water of the inner life. Its strengthened seedlings will express the cosmic promise, the supreme destiny of all humanity.

*Regent – Consciousness or nucleus in charge of capturing and transmitting the evolutionary impulse to all the particles existing within a certain area and leading them to realization.

"Unveiled Secrets – Ibera and Anu Tea" pp. 27-28

The Awakening of a New Consciousness

You live in a time of awakening.

Your search is not limited to you, but is accomplished in conjunction with others. The search is for the real state of your being.

Do not go back to what happened in the past because if you do so, it will limit your memory. Do not limit your union to the corporeal form or to the appearance of facts.

Your being is in permanent contact with other beings.

The limitation that you encounter at present is not in the Law of Spirit but in a temporary condition of material manifestation.

It is necessary to create an opening for the supraconsciousness in order for the interior and superior being to elevate itself from this identity with the physical body, dissolving the preoccupation with the level already attained.

There is one life after another, one world after another, after the dissolution or abandonment of the physical body.

When you project beyond the physical body then you are the traveler of a new mind. In this state, all the unknown circumstances and effects start to manifest themselves in you. In this projection to outside of the physical body, pay attention to not fall into idolatries. Project yourself to the interior of your being, where there is Light that reflects itself to the exterior.

In doing so every group and each individual will understand that the superior values are not the values of the three dimensional world.

Change your state of consciousness, change.

"Miz Tli Tlan – An Awakening World" pp. 150-151

Aggressions Committed by Humanity of the Surface

There are great aggressions committed by the humanity of the surface.

1. Liberation of uncontrollable energy, which is subjecting our and the planet's life to great calamities.

2. Contaminating of the waters of the planet with very little drinking water remaining for our own consumption.

3. With pesticides, fungicides and herbicides, committing the same mistake as was made with nuclear energy, because we cannot control the degree of contamination that is generated when combating plagues. Humanity lacks any idea of the unknown diseases that it will be confronted with that

are produced by environmental contamination. If it was not for the intervention of our great laboratory-spaceships that are working to control the changes that the Earth endures from the release of deadly forces, this civilization of surface would be suffering still more than it suffers today.

But, although bad actions have become very common, yet there are always innocent people who are protected and saved by the Laws of Creation and of Evolution of the races.

"Miz Tli Tlan – An Awakening World" p. 165

Karmic Accounts

Great changes begin to take place when we surrender to a higher level of existence. As our state of consciousness expands we enter a more general karma and begin to be governed by a destiny that is the interplay of various higher destinies. It is no longer our individual karma that now prevails in what happens to us, but rather the interplay of the karma of groups, nations and even of the planet. Our lives become integrated with more powerful forces and we go beyond the sphere of personal limitations.

I know of persons who were in great material need and this need was met when they began to dedicate themselves unselfishly to the spiritual path and to serve through altruistic groups. I know of others who were liberated from personal karmic ties to serve in the wider spheres, such as a country or the planet. Persons who had once been bound by basic duties and confined by family circles suddenly found themselves undergoing transformation and becoming released so that they could dedicate time and energy to universal causes. This does not mean denying the value of duties to be fulfilled, even on the most restrictive and personal levels. Karmic debts can be adjusted and new conditions can arise, setting even indispensible persons free to take on greater tasks.

"Beyond Karma" - Trigueirinho. Irdin Editora, p. 33
(English edition)

Family

Families tend to stimulate the egocentric aspects of their members, to foster self-fulfillment, to exalt self-centeredness and to impose ties of mutual obligation, especially among parents and children, often in a disguised manner. Because of this, families frequently curb the freedom that their members need in order to follow their destined paths.

Ideally the family institution should carry out the role of the first teacher, preparing the incarnating beings to discover their own inner guidance and to recognize the part that they are to play in the progress of the world. However, the family is generally incapable of fulfilling this role and incarnating beings find more hindrance than help in their quest for universal realities within the realms of the family's affection and spirituality. Currently, institutions such as the family, religion and the state, which were created to assist inexperienced souls, are disintegrating. Deprived of this backing, one has to rely on an earnest desire to attain spiritual life so as to be able to follow the quest on one's own and with minimal support.

The family, as an institution, carries a heavy karma. This karma is difficult to resolve while family members remain tied to levels of affinity or rejection that cause various problems in their interrelationships. Moreover, for many, the family group as a social unit has lost its meaning.

However, great and radical transformations await us. The present seemingly hopeless situation will be changed. The new form of relationship that is emerging will be based on interaction among souls and no longer on purely human affinity or rejection. In the forthcoming world cycle other significant changes will also occur in the very constitution of the human being.

"Beyond Karma" - Trigueirinho. Irdin Editora, p. 41
(English edition)

The Law of Detachment

The law of detachment brings flexibility to formal life and increases one's receptivity to soul energy. Through successive detachments from what has already been accomplished, beings become able to express the reality to which they correspond. This is one of the laws of ascesis because to advance on the path an individual cannot take anything with them. However, few can live free and detached. Most are afraid of being without the material bonds to which they are accustomed. Newness frightens them and because of this they distance themselves even when it is near and within reach of everybody.

As one follows the spiritual path the task of detachment acquires deeper connotations and it becomes necessary to dissolve the human links of the traveler. Renunciation is performed by good and altruistic people, but detachment is a more profound attitude. Whoever renounces continues to be involved with the object of renunciation, whereas when one is detached what happens is reminiscent of Jesus' apostles when they were called and they left their boats behind. As a great saint from the past said, "they cut the tie that fastened the boat and didn't distract themselves trying to untie it." Therefore, the law of detachment prevents a setback in the being's evolution.

"The Path of Fire" p. 135

Superior Knowledge

The analytic mind can imprison the individual in that which they already know. By manipulating that which is familiar to oneself it moves us from one comparison to another and in an unstoppable deductive activity, looses the seeds of true reality.

Superior knowledge cannot be explained. Like pure water that comes from within the rocks, it originates in deep springs. Like the wind that penetrates through a crack in the window, it emerges in the consciousness and overtakes the being. It does not announce its arrival, nor says farewell. An unusual traveler, one never knows when it will return.

You can recognize its approach and you can leave open the door. However, it will decide the moment of arrival and without any notice, it will leave again until one day it will take you with it and in the cosmic heights you will live in its dwelling.

After the first encounter, you will not forget it. Even if you take another detour, distracting yourself temporarily with outside movements, it will return to knock at your door and, in every encounter, even if fleeting, will build a bridge that one day you will use to reach the level that will definitely carry you to the Sacred Voyage to the Inner World.

"Mirna Jad – Inner Sanctuary" pp. 140-141

The Way to the Path of Healing

The one who walks, loves silence. The one who walks, loves solitude. The one who walks, follows the course of the law. The one who walks, communes with the hearts of their fellows. The one who walks, forgets about themselves. The one who walks, loses themselves to the world. The one who walks, anchors themselves exclusively in faith. The one who walks, integrates themselves in the Great Chain. The one who walks, becomes themselves the redeemer for their brothers and sisters. Cure is your path. Assume this gift and sow it with gratitude.

Many beings are destined to work as instruments for healing at this time of transition. However, due to the choices they have made, they keep themselves in the initial stages and so they will not be able to act in accordance with what was expected. There are those who persist among them, some are already active and who are as terminals of the sublime chain anchored in the concrete strata of the material sphere. Intense is the work of Our Fraternity. There is no temporal or spatial limit for Our work. The convocation is permanent, and for this the student should not lament for past faults, but advance with tenacity. The portals of Aurora open themselves two by two for those who bring into their centers the seal of truth. The shine of the celestial spheres attracts the most beautiful currents. The cosmic magnet responds to the call. Do not doubt that everything is for the Best.

The truth is a hidden flame in the interior of beings. The Teaching shelters within itself this fire, therefore each one recognizes in it their proper path. Cure corresponds to the strengthening of this flame and to the radiation of its light in the several levels of the being. Therefore the healer does not impress himself with the form, but opens the chains.

The ascension is the path of the chosen ones. In a fiery spiral, the latent silence awakens and penetrates each level of the being, burning obstacles, tearing veils. It is beautiful to see the rising of the fire, it is beautiful to see the answer of the light. Consciousness receives in itself the infinite. The infinite is the pulsation of the unity. In this way, consciousness integrates itself with its Hierarchy.

It is beautiful to see the ascending movement of the fires. By acting as a healer, the being transforms itself into an ardent pyre, returning to the infinite.

In service lies the key to Instruction and it is also the portal for larger universes. Many remain, waiting to be prepared to be able to serve and do not realize that it is service that would prepare them for the new steps. We are referring to ardent service, to the abnegated surrender of the being to evolution. It is like the archer who throws an arrow into the distance. In the fiery tension the server throws himself into the infinite. There are no limits for those who, decisively, embrace the call.

"The Formation of Healers", pp. 38, 92, 93 and 94

Fundamental Activities with Money

Humans have established three fundamental types of activities with money, gold and material goods: the first is buying and selling in which material goods are exchanged for money or for gold; the second is lending money, gold and material goods to someone who is obliged to pay it back; and the third activity is donation to others.

From the spiritual point of view, of these three ways of dealing with money, those with gold and with material goods have different values. In the first the participants do not create ties among themselves if the transaction pleases everybody and is considered fair by them. In the second, the one who lends is linked karmically with the activities that the other one develops to be able to pay the debt. The methods used to earn what one needs to pay back enters into the karmic "account" of both, of the one who borrows as well as of the lender. The third method is the only one that we can say is within the spiritual law, if we examine the topic rigorously without compromises with the involutionary forces that are already at the end of their hegemony on Earth. If there are no attachments by the donor and if there is an opening of heart by the beneficiary, links are not created. Donation is then the freest form for dealing with money or for doing good, if it is done with the correct attitude.

This is also possible in the other two modes of relationship in the absence of attachments or of any other interior compromise. However in these cases, without doubt there is always some participation of collective karma, even if a minimum.

A donation that is completely free and without conditions or attachments on the part of the donor (not even with regards to gratitude) is a way of dealing with goods that is nearer to a spiritual vibration and to the superior laws. The first two ones, although correct with regard to the laws of the surface of Earth, violate larger laws. In reality, goods should belong to everybody and therefore, buying, selling and lending are characteristics of civilizations that do not yet know the true order of the universe.

"The New Beginning of the World" pp. 67-68

The Mind and Evolutionary Work

The common mind does not have access to the internal life. The collective mind of humanity at present is a field of friction and conflict where the involutionary forces are loose. The Hierarchy cannot descend to this level because disharmony is so great that its light would be disintegrated.

In order for our mind to be able to support the evolutionary work, it is necessary to take care of it. Otherwise, there will be a permanent split between the mind which has rebelled, which does not understand, does not agree and which resolves to act on its own, and with the Hierarchy that works in supramental levels.

One way to include the mind in the process of spiritual elevation, one which the heart has already experienced, is to study sacred topics. To read spiritual teachings and to reflect on them, to systematize the knowledge transmitted by the Hierarchy, to relate concepts of several schools of spiritual thought, identifying what they have in common and what is most elevated, are practices that can help the mind to not deviate itself from the path and to not become an obstacle for spiritual growth.

Another possibility for mental work is the constant remembering of the Spiritual Self that lives in our interior. If during the day while doing concrete tasks one remembers to remember and reverence the Spiritual Self, we will begin to establish a connection with it and we will open ourselves to still higher contacts.

We can also remember frequently the inner Hierarchy of the Earth and intend that it will do a work on us. In order to keep the mind occupied with this topic we can, among other things, read about it, listen to talks on the topic, pray, and reflect on the qualities of a certain Hierarchy that inspires devotion in us.

"How to Work Spiritually with the Mind" pp. 55-57

The Inner Key

When human beings enter the world of matter, they bring the key of their cosmic origin concealed within themselves. The history of humanity has been, and continues to be, painful because this inner key has remained forgotten even though it has always been accessible.

Unrestricted and unconditional faith in the existence of a supreme intelligence above all things, is one of the means to discover this key, for it opens the way to awareness of immortality. This kind of faith holds subtle energies that lead a person to live a life in accordance with laws that are above the material ones.

Karma is gradually transformed when one changes one's attitudes. However, the real transformation of karma is based on this faith and on the support of the Hierarchies who inspire humans to fulfill cosmic designs in outer life. As this transformation takes place, one is increasingly liberated from compulsory physical, emotional and mental ties and can enter incarnation with clearly defined purposes, such as to serve the Plan of Evolution.

As we grow in consciousness our understanding of the law of karma changes. We cease considering the law of karma merely as an instrument to compensate for past errors and begin to recognize it as an infallible and extremely useful means to fulfill the higher goal of life.

"Beyond Karma" - Trigueirinho. Irdin Editora, pp 59-60.
(English edition)

The Art of Weaving

Three brothers went to the desert to learn with Zamir the art of weaving.

Zamir lived alone, but his work was known in all the continents. His art, born from silence and solitude brought to people the balms of elevation and cure.

Even knowing that Zamir had never accepted a disciple, the three decided to go in search of this prodigious master. Arriving at the door of his home, the oldest said:

"Oh Great Master, we have traveled for many days and many nights to learn with you the art of weaving. Can you receive us?" From inside one could hear the voice of Zamir.

"I ask you then, why do you want to learn this profession?"

Glad that their words had reached Zamir, the oldest of the brothers hurried himself to answer:

"I want to portray in the material the beauty of morning and the shine of the stars, and to bring others the glory that Nature is imprinted with."

Then the second brother also expressed his aspirations:

"Zamir, I want to weave garments of warriors and priests, of governors and of sages so that they will fulfill their tasks with more glory and splendor."

When a third answer was not given, because the youngest brother remained in silence, Zamir inquired: "And the third of you, why did he come to Zamir?"

And the youngest then replied:

"In Truth, Master, I came to greet you. I do not search for myself. I know that wherever I will be placed by the wise hands of Life, there will be my field of service and work. I will leave now to return because I don't want to take your time. I came to you because I knew that I had to do this and to offer you my humble greeting."

Zamir said to the three:

"The first and second can return. You still have to learn much from life to be able to express the real art of weaving. But to the third one I say: the door of this house is open. Come in because you already know the first lessons of this art: the forgetting of yourself, surrender and service. Come because to you will be revealed the secret of the right tension of the threads and the correct mixture of colors, and to you will be unveiled the mystery of the Great Loom."

"Travel through Subtle Worlds", pp. 117 and 118

The Quietude that Contains All the Answers

It was getting late when a group of seven young aspirants arrived at the ancient monastery, coming from the land of Eicon. They were received by an old monk who welcomed them in the inner patio. The first youth asked:

"O master, when can we have God in our heart?" The monk said to him:

When you have no luggage to carry." The second youth asked:

"Lord, what is the destiny of humans?" The monk answered:

"When the fire burns, the light is one with the clarity of the times, the smoke spreads itself in the air and the ashes stay on the face of the earth."

Without totally understanding this reply, the third youth asked a question hoping for more clarity about what had been said. "And when can we, Lord, no more belong to this Earth?"

The monk answered:

"When you no longer need the food it offers. While it gives you nutrition, your life will be controlled just as, in the business world, you receive according to the credit you have. New times will come however, and for this you will need to have the right garments to enter them."

The fourth youth asked:

"Lord, what garments are these?" And the monk then clarified:

"You carry within yourself the note that you correspond to, but in order for it to be heard it will have to be transformed into sound. Humanity as a whole also has its note. The note of humanity in different periods determines a Race, and its garments are the pattern of behavior and consciousness that it expresses.

As humanity lives a phase of intense transformation, the note it brings elevates itself up the scale and the sound that you will start emitting will be more subtle. Groups of supreme consciousness, of angels and of elemental beings weave this new garment that you will receive.

In each phase the note unveils itself through a scale, but the quality that is in the center of this scale and that created it can only be contacted when you are integrated into the emptiness that is totally unknown to you."

The sun set itself in the horizon, leaving seven brilliant trails that cut the twilight of colors in the sky. The vibration of the monastery was conducive to reflection, but the fifth youth took himself to the old monk, saying:

"I couldn't understand, Lord, what are these notes." The monk said:

"Just as the sun, which you no longer see, shows to you seven of its rays so also in the universe are seven paths to reach the Source. Each one of them determines a note, a Hierarchy and an aspect of the Supreme manifested in creation."

The sixth youth asked:

"How can we come to know the essence of these paths?" The aged one answered:

"In the same way that you cannot know God in His plenitude, but only in the aspects in which He manifests Himself, so you cannot contain the complete essence of these notes, of these paths. Through many means you can bring yourself close to them, and you will discover yours when the love for silence surpasses the desire to know."

Having been silent the whole time, the seventh youth approached himself to the quietness that contains all answers and, so, he had nothing to inquire.

"Travel to Subtle Worlds" pp. 125-127

To Reach the Goal

Not wanting to live anymore that which was destined for him, Saki, the young prince, asked permission from his father to leave on a journey in the direction of other lands.

With great disappointment, but knowing that he could not deny this request, the King gave Saki three presents: a horse, a coat and a small pair of scissors. Even though he did not understand the reason for the last present, Saki accepted the three because he did not want to further upset the old King. He left.

He crossed the frontiers of the kingdom and walked on unknown trails. The coat he received from his father protected him against the coldness of the night, the horse took him agilely through the paths. However, the scissors were of no use.

After a lot of travel, crossing villages, rivers and valleys, Saki found himself facing a large mountain, and in the middle of the woods that covered it, he made out a trail that would take him to its top.

Quickly he entered into it. However, before reaching the first level of stone, half of the way, his horse broke its hoof and Saki had to continue on foot.

Without being discouraged, he continued on the narrow trail. He did not think about the kingdom he had left nor about the experiences on his journey. He only wanted to reach the top of the mountain and this goal, without his realizing it, took over his whole attention.

When he had travelled two-thirds of the distance, a strong storm came, causing the erosion of a part of the trail and throwing the coat that Saki had received from his father far away. Without being able to return, there remained for him the opportunity to go ahead, and even though depressed by the events, he continued on his way. Climbing, he arrived at what seemed to be the end, and he saw that he had not yet encountered the highest part of the mountain. There was a very steep part to be climbed, which could only be seen from the elevated point that he had reached.

Even tired, he continued. Neither the cold nor hunger made him retreat. Three steps from his destiny, encountering a snake ready to attack him and frightening him, the youth slipped and his clothes got caught on the point of a rock. Now he could not move and the snake was coming closer.

As the snake coiled itself, preparing to bite him, he remembered the little pair of scissors he had received from his father. Rapidly he cut his clothes, freeing himself and in a jump he reached the top of the mountain.

To his surprise, he found there a cavern, and from its interior there emanated a brightness. Exhausted, the youth resolved to go towards that light.

As he walked, the light transformed itself into the figure of an ancient sage who had lived in the court of his father. Approaching Saki, he held his hands and said:

"We were waiting for you. You have arrived."

"Travel to Subtle Worlds", pp. 27-28

The Tests and the Heir

Without knowing which of his subjects to choose as his heir, a wise King decided, secretly, to bring them together and test them before making a decision.

The first test which he presented to them was with regard to envy. From the twenty and one servants, only fourteen passed it satisfactorily. He then placed them in a test of subtle intrigue, after which only ten were able to continue. The King then prepared for these select individuals a test of persistence and only seven remained with him. Afterwards was a test relating to gratitude and once it was completed, there were three who could continue.

For them the wise King presented a test relating to treason and only two remained. For them finally, came the test of power which was won by the one who seemed to be the most weak.

In the face of a strong storm, it is easier for the small herb to survive, which, slim and flexible, is able to fold itself whereas a great tree with its height breaks in the middle.

"Travel to Subtle Worlds" p. 113

Departures with Joy

With respect to the times that are now occurring, one can state and warn that the changes will cause many places to consider experiences, as called by some religions, "punishment." These experiences are provided by the Law of Purification, according to the needs of each region.

There will be those who will be evacuated silently, those who will disappear without leaving a trace and without time to inform others, who themselves may or may not be translated or taken away. Do not create expectations regarding facts, because everything will be completely new to you.

The evacuation accomplishes itself in the same way as the body dies. Everything happens in silence and with joy, with much joy, even in the disaster areas. While some "die," others leave. Those who "die," being conscious of the process that is happening, also do it with joy; with joy and in silence, without regrets. Those who leave taking the physical body with them do it with the same harmonious attitude, both internally and externally. Within themselves, everybody understands and lives this unusual reality, knowing why they are leaving, through one process or another.

As Christ said, "Abandon everything and follow Me." Thus, one becomes conscious that there exists a parallel world that is calling, into which many will integrate themselves.

Whoever leaves this way will forget this world through which they were passing. Without becoming upset, but understanding that

they are an integral part of the world with which they are now going to collaborate, they accept and become conscious of their own task and wherever they are, they will develop it.

In these moments, you will KNOW that all is well. Although the dissuasive forces might regroup themselves to destroy your peace and the true light that was lit in your consciousness, do not let yourself be influenced by any impression of this kind.

Hold yourself, in any circumstance, in the highest point of your inner being.

As to the application of the Law of Purification, there will be zones that are more virulent as you will perceive by the examples of what is happening on the surface of the universe-Earth. In other areas there will be a purification that will pass almost unnoticed. Still in others, it will occur in an almost immediate way, without any opportunity for the non-rescuable inhabitants to save themselves. The prophetic books that are known and respected by you refer themselves to these things.

But all the areas will be equally controlled and will have a share in the application of the Law of Purification. No one can integrate themselves into the world that they are searching for before washing themselves interiorly. Therefore the task and role of each one is accomplished by trying to liberate oneself inwardly, so that the exterior part will integrate itself definitely into their task, serving in fact in the way that corresponds to it.

"The Fifth Race" pp. 38-39

Times of Reunion

The human being has a cosmic task to go forward with in conformity with the great plan. There are other worlds, other civilizations that someday will be visited, but, before this, the being has to learn how to use other garments. For this the genetic code is being changed in the bodies.

The future evolution will have a new person with a culture that will not take the individual away from the state GOD-MAN. This culture will give her or him an intelligent consciousness that will integrate them for millennia with other civilizations that populate the infinite cosmos with love energy.

The problems being lived today, because of ignorance or excess of density in the human being will be lost in time. The world will start a new cycle and its black past will not prevail anymore.

The being is a unity but at the same time is multiple. The macro-spirit is cosmic but the human being is on the plane of the micro- spirit. Being thus a micro-cosmos that contains the cell of a Greater Man, the macro-cosmos, it is necessary that it expands in the universe. Each inhabitant of the planet Earth has within themselves the cosmic word that identifies them with the larger dimension that was left when coming here. Always when returning to incarnation, the being brings with them the key, although hidden, of their origin. The history of the planet Earth has been painful until now because this inner key has been forgotten in the interior of each person.

This is a time of reunion on all levels. It is a new beginning of the world, after its global purification.

"The New Beginning of the World", pp. 87-88

After Transforming Yourself, Help and Teach Others

Turu, the sailor, having received five coins of gold for his work, disembarked to an unknown land. He had decided to get to know the deserts and the mountains, and according to the guidance he had received, this was the place where his journey should start.

Upon landing, he bought a horse for one coin, and with the horse started the journey. He travelled through villages and cities until he reached the border of a desert. Then he exchanged the horse he had just bought and another coin for a camel and went off on his trip through the desert.

He accompanied caravans of pilgrims and got to know the heat of the sand and the cold of the night, quenching his thirst in the fountains of the oasis, and he discovered solitude. With his mind made up he crossed the desert and arrived at a village near a great forest. There he exchanged his camel and two more gold coins for an elephant and continued journeying.

A long time had passed since Turu landed on the continent and, on his journey, many lessons about life were learned.

On the back of the elephant, he arrived at a cabin of a well-known guide who agreed to help him to climb a Great Mountain, also giving him provisions. However, the guide said that he could take him only to a certain point of his path, after which Turu would have to proceed alone.

This mountain was famous. The legends spoken of say that nobody has ever come back after reaching its peak. Turu accepted the guide's help and together they started the journey until they reached a large plateau of rock. At this place Turu said farewell to him, confirming his decision to go ahead and, with a sign of gratitude, left him his last coin of gold and the elephant.

Days and nights of sun and rain, of heat and cold passed by. Advancing with the skills of a horse, with the persistence of a camel, and with the wisdom and strength of an elephant, finally Turu arrived at the top of the mountain.

Arriving there he found nothing, besides stone, wind and shallow vegetation. However, without giving up he laid himself on a rock that stood in the direction of the north and slept. He slept asking himself how would be the continuation of the trip, because since the beginning, he had been offering himself to the Light that shone within him. He dreamt that a great flash of light descended from the sky and overwhelmed him, taking him beyond these lands and revealing to him the mysteries of creation. As he absorbed this knowledge, this flash of light radiated his body, transforming him.

Upon waking up, Turu saw in front of him a thin Being who handed him a parchment, saying to him:

"Here is the route of your journey. Go back to the world and teach your brothers on the Path of the Encounter." And this Being, just as He had appeared, disappeared.

Turu returned to the familiarity of other people to fulfill his task.

"Travel to Subtle Worlds", pp. 31-32

Diseases

When looked at from a wider perspective, everything has a role in the Plan of Evolution. Within this plan, illnesses come about because of the need to bring order into one's life. Illnesses are an opportunity for human beings to advance and to balance their negative karma.

Beings who are already conscious on the soul level are aware of their evolutionary goal prior to incarnating. Based on this, they program situations that will provide the necessary developmental experiences during the lifetime about to begin on Earth. Since the soul participates in the design of its own program and has the support of forces made available to it by means of the law of karma, the program always takes into account the level of a person's endurance. In this way, a proposed illness is never greater than one's capacity to bear it. An illness only becomes too heavy to bear when the person rejects it or reacts against it.

When an illness that has been programmed before birth appears, one has to muster up enough strength from within to transcend the state of infirmity. This strength, which would not have been rallied without the illness, is not to be used to struggle against the infirmity but to face it intelligently and cooperatively, seeing it as an opportunity to bring about equilibrium. For example, someone who had committed theft, either in the present or in a former incarnation, might have to suffer a chronic illness in the hands. The effort to treat and to adjust patiently to the malady could, in the overall balance of energies, compensate for the past deed.

In order to alleviate pain or bear discomfort, one should resort to the strength that comes from within. Illnesses could then bring about new understanding and hence, new habits.

"Beyond Karma" pp. 45-46 (English edition)

Faith

Faith is a vibrating element inherent in the cells and must be awakened and energized in your three dimensional world. It belongs to a level of greater refinement than the one that you are in now, and it is this that allows the cellular transmutation to occur.

Faith is a subtle luminous element, a projection of supraphysical energies which brings about the link between the material vibration and the immaterial. This is important for the transmutation of the inferior centers and of the cerebral components which are having their energies raised in the rescuable individuals. The brain cells must awaken in themselves Faith, as it is only in this way that they can capture and transmit to others, through the physical and subtle nervous network, the spirit and the power of transcendence.

In moments of tests and in moments in which your bodies are attacked by retrograde forces, this luminescent element is the sustaining base for the cells to not be dominated by them, and to maintain themselves united to the superior level and to rise through aspiration.

The redemption of the bodies is not possible if Faith is not present, at least in a certain proportion.

Faith is the bridge that links the banks of the Great River. It is the key that takes you to the kingdom that awaits you. Calm yourself. Open yourself to Faith, pure and simple, and let yourself be permeated by it.

You must not wait for your brothers and sisters to wake up to the realities that are being shown to you. You must consider that this humanity has gone through a fall and that it is only part of it that is now regenerating itself and which can be rescued. Furthermore, the cerebral cells of many who could be rescued are dull with the material density of their thoughts and desires, and react mechanically to accept the impulses received from the environment.

Do not forget that lies, falsehoods and intentional mistakes are instilled in humans by the degenerative forces. Those of you who are in accord with these actions are entering the path of disintegration.

"The Time of Rescue" pp. 102 and 103

The Keys to Cross the Sacred Portal

For the individual who sincerely aspires to tread the spiritual path, detachment and the absence of searching for supra-sensorial stimuli are fundamental.

The goal must be the enlargement of consciousness and the disposition, with sincere openness, to express patterns of more and more subtle behavior.

By surrender, service, love and gratitude, the consciousness can elevate itself and recognize the greatness that will come to the being after the present planetary purification.

Even if you deny it, Grace returns to knock on your door. Even if you have expelled it from your being in order to worship other values, it comes back. Even if you despise it, involving yourself with that which is in transition, it will always be ready to welcome you.

When you are circled by the agents of the shadows, do not occupy yourself with them directly. Concentrate your attention on the pact with Our Light, which is an incorruptible link in the great cosmic chain. In this way you will remain detached from the reactions of your bodies and will be able to more freely serve as a channel for the silence and the hidden superior energies.

Surrender, surrender and surrender to this energy. It is the master key that is offered to you to cross the sacred portal.

The Cosmos knocks at the door of humans and, through its slits and openings, brings the Light of life to its dark dwellings. It brings the message of the Christic call in the inner being, inviting it to enter into this universe of beauties and mysteries. Then what is within us can surpass its limits and unite itself to what is reflected in the cosmos, transcending formal projections and unveiling itself in the unmanifested face of what is unknown to the mind.

Therefore, humanity has been given three keys:

Love-Surrender, Faith-Balance, Devotion-Ardor.

United they open the portal of liberation.

"Steps for Now" pp. 6, 7, 19, 38 and 41

Understanding the Correct Use of Money

For us to better understand the correct use of money, let us take as a symbolic example the human blood. The blood flows through all parts of the body without exception. It goes down, and is used for the body's metabolism, goes up to the brain, then returns to the heart and circulates in an adequate rhythm, more or less accelerated, according to the situation. And in this way it gives life to the cells of all parts of the body. While performing this circuit, it renews itself as it goes, without becoming more or less, transforming itself continuously. The process of circulation of monetary energy in society can be compared to the human blood. If the blood stops itself somewhere, if it does not reach the cells, what would happen? Just as no other part of the body can live without it, so no individual on the surface of the planet should be without the material energy that it needs.

When the monetary energy does not flow correctly it is as if all blood of the planet were poisoned. A greater intelligence prepares itself to withdraw from it. Since money was created by humans it has congested itself in certain points of the planet, keeping itself in the hands of some individuals who do not permit its circulation except under certain conditions, in this way letting it become gangrenous. In this senile and decadent civilization, one works and performs according to what is indicated on a bill, check, bank note or similar piece of paper, forgetting that this purpose is given by one's own species and does not fulfill any real necessity that one might have. Can money buy peace? Can it buy health? Can it buy development of consciousness? Can it buy real happiness that goes beyond a superficial smile?

"The New Beginning of the World", pp. 35-36

After the Darkness

The growing chaos on the external level of the planet should not be a reason for sadness or discouragement. On the contrary, it indicates the approach of the final moments of a long and obscure night in which the planetary life was immersed. During the various evolutionary phases the individual on the surface of Earth was kept in ignorance by those who represented the involutionary forces with apparently great power. These forces provoked events such as the setting on fire of the Library of Alexandria; the burning of almost all the documents of the Mayan civilization in the 16th century by a Spanish bishop of the province of Yucatan; the expurgation from the Bible of the teachings of Enoch; the invalidation of the historic documents of Apollonius of Tyana brought about by the efforts of the Church, and so forth until today when more subtle methods are used to perpetrate similar crimes. However, it is exactly after the densest darkness that the rays of light will start to appear, announcing a new cycle. We must open ourselves to this premise, because it is one of those which will direct the entry of the being into the so- called Mysteries.

It will not be long before unusual facts occur in increasing frequency throughout the surface of the Earth, revealing the existence of parallel worlds and their inhabitants. For millennia these beings have been silently helping humanity to avoid its self-destruction. However, they are habitually ridiculed in fictional stories spread by means of films and books that instill misrepresentations into the human mentality. This continues to occur because critique and irony are the defense of individuals who are unprepared to face what transcends them.

"Oceans Can Hear" pp. 129- 130

Listen Pilgrim

Whoever fears to lose their own life cannot receive the gifts of eternity.

Whoever fears to not be taken into consideration by others cannot in fullness, merge themselves with the celestial Life.

But whoever surrenders to the Supreme and does not retain anything, understands the call of the stars and, walking the narrow trail of renunciation, reaches the high peaks and portals of redemption.

Subdue your inferior nature and offer yourself in full consciousness to That which gives you Life and allows you to dive into the inexhaustible Source.

Do not desire names, because they imprison the mind, nor have ambition for positions, or you will be linked to the viscous soil that deludes with its fleeting shine.

For you it is still difficult to understand Divinity because it takes nothing for itself and keeping itself free of all forms and of all concepts, it remains immaculate.

If your smallness reveals itself before the immensity of the celestial spheres, understand the silent message that the shine of the stars is trying to transmit to you.

Remind yourself that there is lightness in the flight of small birds. Listen pilgrim, recognize in ephemeral things the mark of immortality. When you move through the world of changing forms, let yourself be permeated by the unchanging reality.

The veil will dissolve itself after your surrender, but you must first recognize the Law. There is no step that cannot be given and no path that cannot be trod by those who revere the Sacred.

Learn from the waves of the sea the completion of the phases; learn from the succession of the seasons the living of the cycles. Learn from the flower purity of surrender and from the group service of the bees. Follow pilgrim, the directions of your Path of Light.

Make yourself deaf to the calls of the world, silence yourself to their outcry, keep yourself away from incorrect acts, close your eyes to profane visions and renounce the taste of that which links you to illusions. If you conduct the senses as a skilled rider, you will awaken hidden faculties -- not for your own delight, but for redemption and service.

These faculties are the lanterns that will show the way for those who have not freed themselves yet; it is through the warm flame that their heart will be heated, awakening them to a fraternal and spiritual life. Continue ardent seeker, make the senses into collaborators of the Lord, and teach them to adore the One.

Remind yourself that your life does not anymore belong to you, remind yourself that you belong to the Infinite.

"We Are Not Alone" pp. 27-30.

Empty Yourself

The individual cannot receive gifts from heaven while the hands are occupied in retaining material things.

Empty yourself, empty yourself in order to find the true riches. Eternity is known by those who do not plan, who do not nourish memories nor who concern themselves about tomorrow.

For many, it is difficult to recognize the need to disconnect themselves from these ties, the affections, and the things that absorb. However, how can the Unlimited be contained in a being that does not surrender itself to the infinite?

The cosmic energy is a pure, renovating energy, the origin of emanations that vitalize Creation. Its flow through a being depends on how much it can allow this energy to penetrate them without deviating it according to their own tendencies. Even if one aspires to not interfere in the flow, to do this is inevitable when there are ties to human levels. Therefore, the energetic potency accessible to a normal human being linked to matter, is considerably less than what is available to a detached person, evolved spiritually.

The contact with the divine energy cannot be transmitted nor taught. Each contact is unique, because perfection never repeats itself. We could talk about this energy, we could throw light on the path to reach it, but each individual has to tread for themselves these trails, learning to not be upset by the sharp rocks spread along them and to commune with the indescribable beauty of its valleys.

"The Visitor- The Way to Anu Tea" pp. 67-68.

The Role of Those Who Know the True Situation of Planet Earth

Individuals who really become conscious of the situation that the planet is faced with are led to review their life, values, goals and purposes. Then they start to search for patterns of superior conduct, in order to obtain an existence in more harmony with everything.

Although many times we may want to fight against the chaos and the forces that generate it, we will notice that conflict and fricative fire tend to increase disharmony. Therefore, we will see the need to act, based on superior laws and vibrations. From this point on we will discover the power of the solar and cosmic fire present in ourselves and in the whole universe. We will recognize the supra-human laws of evolution and will collaborate with the translation of our own energy from the human to the spiritual plane.

For this process to happen requires a certain amount of time and also perseverance, and a group consciousness that is characteristic of the soul, which begins by approaching itself to the individual so that she or he is attracted to join with others with whom they can fulfill the stages of evolution and service. The energy generated in a group thus formed is greater than the sum of that which derives from each of its participants. Therefore, an authentic group is more than just a gathering of individuals. In order to exist effectively it is necessary to have a common impersonal goal and to have been trusted with an evolutionary task. In this way the interaction of its members thus intensifies the positive aspects of all of the whole and is a channel for impulses to flow that are of great relevance in the transformation of the planetary life.

"Oceans Can Hear", pp. 159 and 160

The Relationship of Humanity with Money

The relationship of human beings with money and material goods is in crisis and ready to be deeply transformed. We are already living this transition in the whole planet. Any evolutionary activity at this time would be sufficient to fix systems and economic regimes that one encounters in their final phase of expression. It is for what will be expressed on planet Earth someday that we work and not for what still exists and is being extinguished.

The process that is currently used for the circulation of gold and money is still linked to the phase in which the planet was becoming more and more material, solid and concrete. Now however, is beginning a cycle of progressive refinement that implies a change of behavior of the human being in dealing with material goods. As we know, all planets have a phase in which they gradually materialize until they reach the peak of their density, as has happened to Earth; then another cycle of dematerialization begins until it totally achieves the supraphysical levels of existence, disappearing from the dense physical plane.

The extensive growth of materialism that we can still see today is therefore, linked to this end of the cycle. From now on, the opposite movement initiates itself; its symptoms can already be perceived in many sectors of human life. The growing interest in supraphysical facts, the development of superior telepathy and abstract thinking; the consciousness of the spiritual purpose of the world and of humanity, are already visible.

The conflict between the forces of density, of materialism in all its manifestations, and the forces of the new Earth and the ever increasing link with the supraphysical worlds is already evident. On the subtle levels of planetary life this conflict has already been resolved and there is no struggle, however, in the three dimensions in which the human being is conscious – physical, emotional and mental – it still exists in a way that is very apparent. This still happens because these planes take a long time to reflect the real, superior situation. On the more elevated levels of consciousness, for example, each individual of the surface of Earth has already decided which path to follow: that of the evolutionary or of the involuntary energies. However, on the level of personality people do not have conscious awareness of the choice they made and therefore, still have mental, emotional and even physical-etheric struggles, as can be seen in the precarious state of health that often times manifests itself.

There are still conflicts on the psychological levels of the individual who in their life, does not recognize that having material goods for their own use or only for the use of those who are strictly linked to them karmically is a phase that has been surpassed in the internal planes of their consciousness. Many already have the tendency to use these goods not for themselves anymore, but for the purpose of an evolutionary plan they have begun to envision and know, sometimes intuitively, others through external signs that are very clear.

However, before somebody can really be useful and integrated with a plan of work for the well-being of humanity, it is necessary that they have done some work in the sense of transcending their own desire, their own sensuality and their own common thought. Desire leads an individual to pursue and acquire the superfluous; sensuality makes them interpret life in a materialistic way, and common thought makes them follow formulas, concepts or previous experiences that often no longer serve them, for the Spirit always renews itself and, therefore, does not repeat situations when the lessons taught have already been learned.

"The New Beginning of the World" pp. 73-76

To Withdraw the Senses – This is What You Have to Do

What you can do on your own is to withdraw the senses and to bring back together all your attention on one point and then elevate it into a complete surrender, offering it to the Creator. In order to do so it is necessary for you to consider the Path to Divine Life as the greatest treasure and the most valuable good, because if not, even though you long for the quietness of the senses, they will not obey you when you call them to retreat. The senses normally do not have any interest in the divine life and will not know silence if they do not complete a certain stage of the Path, until they finally discover that this is the true and only destiny.

This silence is necessary. A calm sea is necessary for you to be able to study with serenity the design of the lands that encircle you. This study is not done in schools. The features of these lands will be revealed to you when your boat finally allows itself to be taken to them, where they have been awaiting you for a long time.

So you will perceive that, even if you have been told that the destiny of everybody is to reach these inner worlds, you can only reach them when in your own garments certain works have been accomplished, when they will already have certain vibrations transformed and transmuted. As these states are being transcended an individual detaches from the material aspects to which they were linked by affinity or by vibrating correspondence.

You can see that you will have a lot of work if your essence already lives in unison with the superior planes and with the nuclei of pure spiritual and divine radiation, while you are in service fulfilling specific material stages in bodies that do not correspond to your inner state.

Did you know why you were destined to live this situation? If in your being there emerges the smallest questioning and non- acceptance of all that you have received, you should know that surely this situation remains appropriate in order for you to grow in gratitude, obedience and surrender. If you have not been able to impregnate your material vehicles with these qualities, how can you expect to be freed from the terrestrial planes? We repeat: have you come closer to knowing silence? Not the silence of a muted external, but a silence which is the fruit of surrender, the silence that is the only king on an earth that has offered itself to the Supreme Royalty.

"From Struggle to Peace" pp. 31-32

Three Kinds of Actions

There are three kinds of actions: those performed in relationship to individual duties prescribed by the scriptures revealed in the past: those that liberate the individual from the cycle of birth and death, and those which involve the improper use of individual freedom and that lead to inferior forms of life.

Among these three categories of actions, intelligent persons prefer the ones that free them from slavery. Common people want to do good works in order to be recognized in order to obtain higher positions in this or in the next world. However, those who are more advanced aspire to liberate themselves completely from reactions, even from those generated by their own work. They know that good as well as bad deeds tie them equally to material suffering, and consequently they search to operate in a way that frees them from these works. It is never too much to reaffirm that there is a plan of inner life, a micro-spiritual kingdom integrated with the divine spark of the macro-cosmos that, for its existence, does not depend on any exterior manifestation.

"MIZ TLI TAN - An Awakening World", pp. 76-77

The Student and Prayer

Once upon a time a student, moved by an impulse that left him with no other choice but to obey, kept himself for a period of time in a permanent state of prayer. Sometimes during the day a need spontaneously emerged from within him to place himself in quietness and to offer himself to the energies directing the planetary awakening.

For an unknown reason, in these moments of impersonal prayer there arose inside of him a connection with those who suffer. This student sheltered the pain of these beings as if it were his own, taking into account that when one is touched by the Light, it reveals that everything is passing.

Until this praying process had established itself and also because he did not have full consciousness of what was happening, he was not inwardly permitted to speak about it with anyone. These prayers arose by themselves in each moment that he was able to disengage himself from external activities, perceiving that he should not create any obstacle to them. It seemed to him important to be simply complete in this attitude of surrender and service.

***

In the midst of the current planetary situation, already very critical, aspirants to a superior life who desire to serve are faced with their own limitations, having to consider their human incapacity to recognize the divine leadership and to surrender themselves totally to it.

In reality, no being has the conditions to reach the Light and service by what is available to humankind. To undertake this search, one should repeatedly confirm their faith and trust only in God. Saint Francis of Assisi, faced with the play of negative forces that emerged in the religious Order that he had formed, repeated a phrase from the prophet Jeremiah that said: "dammed is the one who puts his faith in humans."

The majority of human beings still have strong ties with physical matter and consequently with evil. However, even one drop of true Life which falls in the arid terrain of terrestrial existence can act profoundly, bringing closer the time for this earth to be transformed into a fertile soil for the creative impulses of the spirit.

"The Creation (Following the Ways of Energy) pp. 63-64

To Know How to Be Free

The healing of humanity is also the transformation of the way each individual perceives the universe and relates themselves to it. It is a process that demands energy and which itself becomes critical when the being attaches itself to what it was, or has plans about what it should be. But on the other hand, healing follows the path of evolution and in order for it to realize itself, it needs only the opening of our being, because through all of life we receive potent impulses in the direction of the evolutionary goal.

When a being begins this journey, normally it is given external tasks that represent important opportunities. Among other things, they serve for the individual to learn to not make service into a means for self-satisfaction. Therefore, it brings one to pass through many tests in order to reach a state in which it becomes necessary to change the polarization of one's consciousness. When this moment arrives, it is no longer possible to continue relating oneself to the external world through projections based on what has been accumulated since entering into matter, by means of the great personal and hereditary load formed over time. In this moment it is possible that an occult rebirth can occur.

In order for this to take place, the energy tries to undo within the individual the ties that have kept them with the past and with what they were until then. It tries to liberate them as much as possible to bear the emptiness that, in reality, is the cradle of this new consciousness. But the being does not know how to be free. It is more difficult to bring it to freedom than to keep it in the prison of its own concepts. This obtuse reality is the one that still persists in the present world. However, Grace has already started its work and the changes that are going to happen will not allow this situation to continue.

"The Healing of Humanity" pp. 116-117

The Pilgrim and the Serious Man

Once upon a time, walking alongside a pilgrim during a long journey, was a serious austere man with a harsh and grave face. As the pilgrim himself became lighter with each step, leaving behind that which he had been, this man walked sluggishly, turning around his thoughts, and it seemed that what he brought with him was getting heavier. In silence, the pilgrim opened himself to his surrender and to the joy that came from it, so that he might bring help to open the person who, on account of his fixed mental concepts, did not allow the purity of his own spiritual state to emerge. And, little by little, lightness started to introduce itself into the expression of that man.

When a being manifests the joy of communion with subtle energies, its capacity to help those who still do not recognize the need to turn themselves to the light is greater when they do not keep for themselves what the inner life grants them. It is the ardor of the fire that raises the glow of the flame. The healthy, serene joy, full of peace that emerges from the touch of the spirit should not be hidden. Humanity will receive a greater good through the example of union with inner nuclei than by the rigidity imposed by ideas about how the behavior of an evolved person should be. Soberness is necessary and without it clarity will not reach the mind, but it is not incompatible with joy. Both, if real, harmonize themselves in the revelation of a life devoted to the Supreme.

"The Healing of Humanity" pp. 57-58

A New Universe

The dispersion which one can observe today in the world is being balanced by an inner movement that relies on the help of some members of this humanity. In the heart of beings and of material particles, a new universe is being constructed and when this civilization will achieve its complete ruin, many will recognize – within themselves – that a new life is ready within them. For these, the change will be a natural step, without resistance or opposition.

When the moment of encounter with this new life arrives, its patterns will silently penetrate the consciousness. They will enter without being noticed, establish their bases and radiate renewing energies. And so, without any apparent reason, the individual who is touched by this life discovers that he or she can no longer continue to act according to habit as they did before. Without knowing how, they become receptive to what they have often denied. And without having done anything, they recognize that another being flourishes within themselves, more conscious, more balanced, and one that shares a universal harmony. Their existence is absorbed in the spheres of a larger life. They turn themselves to the coming manifestation with multitudes of pilgrims. Lines of light form themselves from the ardor and joy that emanate from them. They go to meet that which, even without knowing, they have always aspired to. They have been able to conquer fear and transcend the ideas about what is possible for the being to realize. Over them is a sacred presence. From Above they receive blessings. And, at their side, sublime beings gather themselves.

Wise are those who find themselves and from their deepest center obtain the signs that they need. They grow in serenity and balance. They do not want to reach any point, nor remain where they are. They do not interrupt their journey, but are not anxious to arrive at the end of it. They are ruled by continuous supramental laws and discover that although there exist infinite possible routes, only one is the perfect one.

"The Healing of Humanity" pp. 83-89

The Miracle

A miracle is the penetration of the new into the consciousness of beings and of the planet. It is the fruit of an opening that cannot be limited and through which unusual and healing energies introduce themselves. A miracle is the pure materialization of the supramental reality, the rupture of illusion and the withdrawal of the veils, letting the truth be revealed.

A miracle is this complete possibility for an immaterial law to express itself, of a superior purpose to express itself on the planetary surface, where the laws of the concrete life still rule the being and its rational mind.

Miracles are normal in a life linked to the inner world, because it does not have limits between will and manifestation, between essence and form. The unification existing between the energies that circulate in the inner levels allows the life present in them to be harmonious in action and also to be a creative and dissolving power, because it is beyond the forms that it assumes to do the work.

The being should allow for a state of transcendence and detachment to spring up in it. It is necessary that one disconnect from the transitory and ephemeral so that reality can spring up to become the leader of concrete life and to be able to do its work of unifying worlds. Every formal creation is ephemeral, but in essence contains the eternal. So there is a delicate balance to be found by the being in a relationship with the material world: to mold life according to the divine idea without however binding oneself to temporality and without allowing oneself to be deceived by the form.

"The Healing of Humanity" p. 61

Humanity Today

Today the impossibility that a process of deterioration of life on the surface of the planet can be reversed by human action has led humanity to a situation of great inner and outer conflict. The maturity that has not been assumed for centuries will have to be consummated in a short time in an operation guided by intelligent cosmic energies. However, a majority of people have not allowed themselves to be prepared for this maturity, keeping themselves closed, confirming habits, tendencies and aspects that belong to immature stages of their evolution.

As this is indispensable for the entering of the whole planetary life into an adult phase, conscious of its role and of its importance for the equilibrium of the universes, humanity cannot remove itself from it. Due to the resistance of humanity to transcending its identification with common, material life, this transition will take on the aspect of suffering, pain and conflict.

This picture may seem lacking in joy for those who feel comfortable, but it arouses in those who are ready an anxiety to serve, realizing what is necessary for the elevation of the quality of terrestrial life. It is in these conditions that the biggest opportunities of inner growth offered up until now, are making themselves accessible to humanity. But few notice what is really happening. Those who are conscious have a duty towards those who are in obscurity, because some of them will still awaken before a more acute state of chaos than that which exists at present installs itself.

Each individual must recognize their own task and not measure efforts to fulfill it. One must perceive and make the necessary changes to accomplish it and keep oneself attentive to not put restrictions on what one must do.

There is a mistake that beings must dissolve: the illusion that the experience of new energies or superior realities is only possible in reclusive, closed, monastic environments. It is necessary to have individuals in retreat in such areas but it is especially necessary to have others tuned with the light in large cities. It is not worth establishing outer values for these situations. What is important is to be clear about the task that corresponds to each one and to live it without conflict, without expectations and without dispersing oneself in dreams or mental creations that only deviate consciousness from the goal.

This is the moment to transcend the vibrating state of this humanity, where comparisons are still made and where it is believed that one work is less valuable than another one. The dignity of a task is mirrored by those who, by carrying it out, are fully conscious of the need to fulfill it and devote themselves to it with unlimited love. Thus, any and every work, wherever it is done, can reflect the sacred.

"The Visitor (The Way to Anu Tea) pp. 63-64

Extreme Times

The present times are characterized by a coming and going of contrasts and violence. We are in a time of extremes, of discoveries of service to power and to extermination. Atomic, bacteriological and chemical weapons are maintained by humanity while at the same time in the sky arise channeled lights that bring them cosmic messages.

When an individual ceases to limit themselves to external manifestations of these messages, discarding as well the spurious interest for phenomenon that accompanies it, the occult side of realities reveal plans that are immediately perceptible, developing in the individual the capacity of contacting them. Then one finds oneself before a science that, while exact, has innumerable variants and is always in evolution. The maintaining of an internal and external mental attunement fixed on a purpose allows for the awakening within oneself of an uninterrupted fluency of knowledge.

The knowledge that today is arriving to humanity, determines for it the nature of a reality that can no longer be denied, because its evidence appears in our skies, giving more light to the rebirth and bringing a new language and new gifts from the cosmic Hierarchies. Humans try to project themselves towards other planets in order to conquer them, when lives and superior civilizations are already here, visible and close. They move themselves in different worlds than ours, that is, in planes organized in another way, and guided by Love.

"MIZ TLI TAN, An Awakening World" pp. 103-104

The Law of Purification

The Law of Purification is presented for the universes that are inhabited by races of the surface. The surface terrestrial race, for example, has forgotten its origin and confused itself with the solid body. While it speaks about the soul and the spirit, which is its true nucleus of life, of energy, of action and of movement, it embraces everything that is material and it forgets the divine essence, the part of the Cosmos that lives in the inner being as it also does in all the other races. It has lived by the most illicit means from the perspective of the cosmic laws of love, and it has turned itself aggressive. It has even violated the natural laws that are the means of life and of purification of the dense vehicles that humans are formed of.

The Law of Purification is that which allows the being to return to its source, to its cosmic origins, that brings it to respect larger laws and to live within harmony. It leads the being until it leaves the law of birth, death and karma present in dense matter. The distraction of those who embrace the dense and the material brings about the necessity of a cyclic application of this law of planetary mutation in the four kingdoms of the three dimensional world.

The Law of Purification is subject to the Evolutionary Law of the four realms and to the laws that govern each realm, as well as to the laws of the planet to which it is applied. It is established for the civilizations that inhabit the planets still in their evolutionary state, and not for those that have completed certain cycles of the Divine Law. A law can become severe when civilizations deviate themselves from the divine plan. Therefore, the Law of Purification is love and justice within the laws that form the life of the universes.

"MIZ TLI TAN, An Awakening World" pp. 170-171

The Feminine Polarity

Until 8.8.88 masculine positive traits predominated on Earth. From that date the regent energy started to express its feminine side, its qualities of receptivity and of refinement. One of the important aspects of the evolution of human beings, an aspect that is now coming to be stimulated, is the development of the right-side consciousness. The energetic circuit of the chakras corresponds to the expression of the masculine planetary polarity and, remaining under its laws is not then a goal of those who follow the evolutionary rhythm that is presently impressing itself on the life on Earth.

The feminine energy by its nature induces the being to recollection. It does not have as a fundamental trait the impulse of exteriorization, but rather of inner action. Therefore, the interaction with the Intra-terrestrial Centers and with the inner worlds of the Cosmos will be greatly facilitated in this stage.

It is worth remembering that the polarities are present in all of the manifested universe, whether it be in the macro-cosmos or in the micro-cosmos. Therefore independently of the kind of body being used by a being in the concrete material world, they possess in their essence the two poles of energy and can express the sublime qualities of both when serving the superior purpose of evolution. Besides, when one says that a planetary polarity awakens or enters into activity, this refers itself to the regency of a certain planetary cycle and to the characteristics of the evolutionary processes in this cycle. In truth, the different grades of the two polarities are always acting, leading the beings and life to unification in levels that transcend the opposites.

"Oceans Can Hear" pp. 149 and 150

For Those Who Have Decided to Serve the Planet

Today more than ever, an adequate discipline which does not attack others and which attracts little attention is necessary. It is a matter of having a discipline full of joy and sense of responsibility. With it we have open doors to greater steps. However, "beware of the ones who scattered the seeds of the world in their own garden – because joy is for the one who gave out each seed of comprehension to the Common Good." This is the call for all who have decided to serve the planet. This is a principle for living the Service within the Spiritual Law.

So extensive is the work on this planet – an evolutionary work – that all the possible forces are necessary and must be gathered for this purpose. Everyone, without the exception of anyone, can be one of the builders of the coming future. There is work for everyone, in all the degrees of ability and quality of intention. Humanity finds enthusiasm and time for so much degrading work, but it is time to change this and for humanity to dedicate itself to dignified work.

We all know that the plans for the New Earth and the New Humanity are pleasing almost exclusively to the simple souls. The Teachings point out that "on the eve of a catastrophe, we tried to lead the people to the outside of an amusement park. Not only did the people not leave, but the crowd still tried to get in."

This is the normal reality, and those who dedicate themselves to education, or who include themselves in the task of rescuing of souls will encounter it before them. But it is knowingly said that it is the solitary spirit that provides the future shape of life. Do not find it strange, therefore, if we find ourselves alone. And why do so many avoid the unusual, the unknown? Could it not be because they are encouraged in schools to live like the majority?

Signs of Blavatsky, An Unusual Encounter for the Present Time. Trigueirinho. Irdin Editoria, pp. 59-60 (English Edition)

True Prayer

True prayer is a state of complete internal serenity and you enter into it when you no longer become engaged with the involvements that come to you. So great will be your dedication to this path that you would not take your eyes off it, not even for a moment, as there are many forces that try to hold you back so that only a moment of distraction would be enough for you to go off on a side-track that will distance you from the Goal.

If you want to reach this Inner Dwelling, so pure that you will perceive it only when you are unable to stain it anymore, observe your baggage and relieve it of that which weighs most and that which can attract the most dust and dirt, so that you may continue with the part that corresponds in quality to the destiny you are led to.

The tasks that are given to you, insofar as you are able to fulfill them, will be larger if you are able to endure greater tribulations, and smaller if your faith, donation and love are smaller. Because for those who offer themselves to live in the name of the Law, there are no resistances and tests that can impede them from going forward. And the more is the love that you have for the inner life, the more you will be able to bear the tests and affirm it to the world, because they will make you strong and this firmness, as incredible as it may seem from the point of view of the skeptical people, will be the proof of your existence.

If you are not ready to allow the Superior Will to accomplish itself through you, you will have a life appropriate to this partial surrender. But if you have the capacity for a total surrender, the Will will be done. If you have to endure, you will endure not with suffering but with a sense of plenitude for you will know that you are fulfilling that which your inner being asks you for. One can say to you that there is no earthly joy that surpasses the peace of this state.

The kingdom is not arrived at by force or through an effort nurtured by pride and by human vanity. The path to the spirit is the path of the pure, the simple and the humble ones, of those who know they can do nothing on their own and that there is nothing of truth that is not their own Consciousness. It is the path of those who in the silence of recollection turn themselves to the Absolute: "Thy will be done!"

Even if you feel grateful for this Will, you must know that you have nothing and for this the divine consciousness takes nothing from you. If you really come to know this Love, only with your surrender will you be able to repay all that has been given to you.

Thus, it is also important to know how to receive and that with humbleness you do not let yourself worry about not having something with which to show your gratitude. If you really are grateful, the peace and plenitude that will radiate will be the most valuable thing that you can do with what has been given to you.

Take care also to not close the doors to where you have been brought by the spirit, thinking that you are not deserving. Instead of real humbleness you will notice that these attitudes are daughters of arrogance, a consequence of believing that first you need to be ready, rather than being in a place of surrender and allowing to be done in you what has to be done.

"From Struggle to Peace" pp. 203-204

To Divinize Matter

A new energetic situation is hovering in the skies of this planet that is no longer possible for conscious human beings to deny. It is necessary to divinize it and this cannot be brought about by placing a cover of perfection over the external life, when underneath everything is deteriorating. In order for the wounds to heal, one must not hide them. A potent energy tries to materialize itself.

This is a moment in which superficial changes are not useful. It is time for deep transformations in which decisions confirm themselves and true steps bring themselves about.

In the middle of this stage of transition, one of the foundations that this humanity has relied on and which cannot continue to survive, is the traditional family structure. The emanations of the Cosmic

Fraternity permeate this planet, and in consequence of this renovating impulses update the terrestrial life. Inner freedom has to overcome social patterns, concepts and collective tendencies that limit the pure expression of consciousness.

It is necessary to transcend what the past has instilled in beings, in the mind, in matter, in the fundamentals on which this civilization is based. The true expression of fraternity, today unknown to humanity, will only turn itself into a concrete reality when the links of terrestrial humanity with a Hierarchy are firmly established.

Beings who perceive the need for these links to establish themselves work in order to create a space for it. However, the life that is destined for the surface of Earth is still waiting for a greater opening to realize itself. Do not nourish and confirm stagnation and the perpetuation of what is no longer valid for humans. It is necessary to let the new energy throw off its sparks of fire, consuming old schemes and purifying areas of consciousness so that in them the truth can emerge.

"The Healing of Humanity" pp. 123-124

Where to Place Thought and Aspiration

An important key within spirituality is to dedicate not only our idle time to the search for attunement with the Higher, but to really pervade all of our life with this aspiration.

A little yoga story tells us about a dark spirit who thought: "How may I tie humanity more firmly to the Earth? Let them keep their usual habits and customs. Nothing is as binding to humanity as ordinary images." So, for this, the dark forces labor tirelessly.

But to where should we direct our will, which is so powerful and unknown to the majority, and where should the thoughts and aspiration be placed? At the same time that we focus on our inner part we should learn to head towards infinite space, towards superior worlds and towards beings who have already passed beyond our present stage and await the slightest sign to attune with us and instruct us on matters of the Universe.

An important key within spirituality is to dedicate not only our idle time to the search for attunement with the Higher, but to really pervade all of our life with this aspiration.

"Signs of Blavatsky, An Unusual Encounter for the Present Time" pp. 50 (English edition)

To Learn to See

Every theory constitutes a faithful reflection of the state of consciousness of its creator. With the process of development of the being, always new and different theories start emerging successively. They are, in reality, the fruit of a unique universal creation that generates new forms while the previous ones turn out to be insufficient.

So, the truth of today can be an untruth tomorrow. A retrospective vision of the past of humanity confirms this fact. Therefore, it is almost impossible to judge what is told by history. The history of science, for example, is the history of human mistakes. There is no reason for us to be ashamed of this; we must know that through mistakes much is learned. The grotesqueness of human behavior resides in the fact that each generation, even perceiving the mistakes of the previous one, deceives itself into believing that it is right. It is this arrogance that hinders one from seeing clearly; the cosmic teachings maintain themselves secret from those who do not enter a more universal state of consciousness.

The individual who has not studied physics cannot understand certain formulas, no matter how important they are for science. However, acquiring the necessary knowledge these formulas become meaningful to them. The same happens to cosmic truths that the new humanity needs to know.

The codes of these truths are accessible to everyone; nevertheless, they cannot be recognized by the ignorant. The great mass of humanity does not perceive, for example, the value of symbols. To SEE it is necessary to LEARN TO SEE. "The Light approaches the darkness, but the darkness comprehends it not."

"The Space Gardeners" pp. 67-68

Inevitable Conflicts

With each change of cycle the energetic voltage that permeates the planet elevates itself. This process reflects itself in each living being and, especially at present, facilitates the approach of monadic energy to the outer consciousness of individuals, bringing transformations in all the levels of existence. These restructurings demand adjustment in the being and many times provoke conflicts. In these moments, it is necessary to have patience with oneself, as well as compassion and love-wisdom, energies that are part of the art of living.

If in the inner levels of an individual there is the decision to take on a strictly spiritual life, with purity, then while seeking to realize it one might face resistance within themselves from the conscious I and from the bodies. When these resistances emerge the links that the matter of the bodies have with negative forces bring about distortions in behavior. However, if the conscious I recognizes its limitations and makes an effort to surrender itself, a purification takes place, a preparation required for the total cure that may occur later.

It is not recommended to keep the attention on one's own difficulties. According to spiritual law, the Supreme Will knows before we do, that which is necessary. Urgent is the need of surrender and vigilance. This way one can proceed without many mistakes. The inner help is always available and, thanks to it, in many moments it is possible to not allow oneself to be overcome nor to permit the energy to be dispersed.

This help comes to meet the being in an indescribable way if there is persistence in one's ascesis. Even knowing that perfection is distant from what is being expressed, we should trust the manifestation of divine life and go forward without being knocked down by the falls.

"The Birth of Future Humanity" pp. 52-53

Falling Asleep Correctly

When we lie down and prepare ourselves to fall asleep, the superior I comes to gather all the available energies, bringing them to the region of the cardiac center. It is important to accompany this movement, interiorizing ourselves and setting out for a calm sleep, in the direction of more profound levels.

When the physical body and the brain sleep, the soul retires itself to its own level, from which it may or may not send impressions to the bodies of the personality. If the bodies are ready and relaxed, the messages of the soul can get through to them. In this way, when the body wakes up after the sleep it will have registered in the brain that which the soul has sent.

If the necessary rest has not occurred, the physical brain will continue to register that which has happened around it and will be prevented from capturing that which happens in the subtle levels during the night.

It is also necessary for the emotional body to be in a state of relaxation. The thinking or concrete mind can also produce dreams of its own accord, because what happens during the day is impressed on it. Because the mental body allows us to act with the will energy, it is only necessary for us to not want to put up with external thoughts, individual or collective.

It would be good if, when going to sleep we quickly reached with consciousness, the deeper zones of our being. There is a technique that can be used. It consists of a special care with the final moment that precedes sleep, a moment in which we enter the dreamlike state. There, the last conscious thought must be positive, imbued with the intention of going to a much higher, superior level. Regarding the habit of reading before going to sleep, the quality of dream life will depend upon the quality of the text. Every reading links us to the mental plane of the writer or to the level where they were inspired.

Another point to be considered is the time of going to sleep. It is good to have a fixed regular time.

The use of these techniques or of others must not be permanent. Obtaining self-control, a person discovers a discipline that is right for them, after which they can receive an inner orientation about it which, at a certain point usually occurs.

"Our Life in Dreams" pp. 31-36

Awakening Correctly

There is a very short moment of perception, an instant when one notices that one is awakening and in which are recapitulated the events of the night. It is at this moment that one must be careful to not allow the entrance of preoccupations or plans about the routine for the coming day. We must try in this moment to be immobile and without any thoughts. Upon becoming silent, one perceives the body awakening and will take care not to move it, especially the head. A simple movement of the head can alter the whole picturing of the dream.

If some part of a dream needs to come to memory, it may come in this special moment. If one remembers only one part, it is only necessary to keep it present so the others can arise little by little. There are cases in which, after waking up calmly the dream comes back to memory all at once and it is not necessary to recapitulate it. Still, one should remain quiet, with all the necessary precautions. When the dream has come to memory, one can take notes before trying to remember another dream that may have occurred in the same night.

After a creative night one will be transformed, especially if the profound sleep was beneficial. There are people who have great ideas when they wake up. For them one recommends that before falling asleep, they see with clarity the matter to be solved and turn it over to the supra-consciousness. By sending it to the deepest part of the being and not thinking more about it, the solution can imprinted itself on the physical brain in the moment of awakening.

In the event that the dream is interrupted by the movement of somebody nearby or by an alarm clock, the consciousness has to return suddenly to inside the body, which can eliminate the possibility for the person to remember what has happened during sleep. Those who use an alarm clock ignore the fact that the physical body has its own consciousness. As it is always active, one must only ask it to wake up the physical body at a certain time and it will cooperate.

Even if one adopts all of these positive attitudes, it is well to remember that the unfolding of the events in the inner level during the sleep of the physical body is not in our control – unless in the case of a common, normal dream, produced by desire, which can be directed if one is well-trained.

"Our Life in Dreams", pp. 37-40

Involutionary Forces

Aggressive events roar through these lands, with the conflicts emerging between brother and sister nations, between parents and children and friends, demonstrating that the involutionary forces are free on the surface of the planet. There have always been fights, but not with the graveness that occurs at present in fights and confrontations between humans. Destructive forces are spreading themselves everywhere, reaching homes, schools and the arts. As you can see, the expression in music, as well as in painting, is lacking in harmony and beauty, and different from the past, when inspired individuals touched the canvas and strings.

Today the race finds itself prey to the unbalance brought by the involutionary forces, and they cause this great confusion about achieving power and control. However, those who search the Light, those who willingly are waiting for the Energy, will not lose control, even if for moments they might find themselves in emotional crises. Many people today cannot control themselves and live dependent on strong medicines, without this achieving a lessening of their crisis – remedies that cannot combat the true cause of the problem.

The involuntary forces have even taken over physical bodies, but this will only be recognized by those who are walking in Light. Those who are lost and disturbed will praise them, confusing themselves. Therefore, one must pray a lot. Keep in vigil and recognize who is coming to get you. THE LAW can also take on a physical body and one will recognize it by its own Light.

Guard yourself from being tempted by your weaknesses, because there will be forces that will try to distance you from the chosen path.

"New Signs of Contact" pp. 125-126

Letting Yourself Be Led by Wisdom

A student had a dream that gave him the impression of extreme misery; it reflected critical moments that await this humanity and that in part are already happening. In this dream he entered a hospital and was attentive to what was going on there. He realized that there was no more room to receive the sick people; they were too many. A large number of debilitated individuals reported there, but at the entrance they were told there was no more space and that several attendants were absent. Two medical offices were without the people in charge and there was so much deprivation that the sick people were moved into these offices because there was no more space in the other parts of the hospital.

When the student woke up, he asked: "What should one do in this situation?" The following answer was given to him interiorly, bringing important impulses to attune with reality.

Open yourself to Wisdom and allow yourself to be led by it. True knowledge will be given to you at the patient's bedside when you assume your task, and not through already established theories or systems. What you need will be given to you. Your instructor will be the task itself; your instruments, the opening and surrender to the service.

You should neither feed on worries about the material consequences of this planetary transition nor focus your attention on diseases or impoverishment of the bodies, even if there is an urgent need. In this period of growing crisis, most people are in a state of precarious balance and need, a need that comes from supraphysical levels. It is when the individual surrenders with no restrictions to the realization of their true task, that everything functions according to a precise and wise order, although hidden in most cases.

Niskalkat (The Etheric Base in Asia)" pp. 35-36
(Unpublished English edition)

A Crucial Moment

The Earth is going through a transition in which cosmic energies, more potent and pure, are starting to permeate it and to remove negative forces that for millennia have been established here.

Consciously or unconsciously everybody knows what they are dealing with when they hear about this transition and right away will perceive that it will transform the whole surface of the planet. They feel tension, fear or depression as their old values start declining. Especially in the cities, the decadent foundations of this civilization take on great dimensions, destroying the mood, the harmony and the balance, impeding the existence of peace between beings and in the interior of each.

But it is possible to be in this planetary transition in an intelligent way, not as a victim, but as a collaborator of the superior, radiant and luminous energies that are starting to implant themselves. For this, it is important to know that thoughts and emotions are generally immersed in this contaminated collective field of tension and conflict and therefore, they are not reliable.

The first step is to have a conscious awareness that in one's own being there is a nucleus that is above all normal thoughts and emotions, a nucleus of stable harmony that does not allow itself to be affected by any external situation. It is about trying to aspire to a contact and to identify with this nucleus.

The second step is to learn how to restrain the mind to impede its tendency to involve itself with the disharmonious stimuli that it receives. These two steps: one, of the recognition of the nuclei of inner peace and second; of the control of the mind, are fundamental. In the face of any conflictual situation these steps have great value.

Another essential step is not to allow inertia to be introduced into the being. Tension and depression weaken the body of energies - what is called the etheric body - which if weakened, can lead a person to apathy. The correct use of the will and the realization of evolutionary activities are indispensable.

People who are passing through an attack of disordered psychic forces or who have been affected by some shock or loss, should neither isolate themselves nor confirm this state, but look to find activities that can possibly help others.

Hygiene, order and harmony in oneself and in the environment are more important than one thinks, because they prevent the entrance of states of chaos. Keep them as a kind of preventive, prophylactic measure, without interruption, because the conflictive forces of the psychic levels sustain themselves on these disharmonies. Along with this, during emotional or mental instabilities, our relationship with food destabilizes itself, and a person can either eat too much in a tendency to compensate for the weakness (which does not resolve it because its cause is not physical), or they may lose appetite due to apathy or lack of interest in life. In any circumstance, simple food without excessive spices, contributes to the regularization of the organic rhythms.

It is also fundamental to always maintain one's independence regarding opinions and ideas that circulate and that most of the time cause confusion. An example is the anxiety that takes place due to the belief that the body's health is lost when one doesn't sleep well. If somebody doesn't sleep well, instead of becoming anxious or distressed, this person should creatively use the time by performing a task and in this way, try to discipline their mental activity. When there is lack of order, it is the person who is the principle cause of insomnia.

A powerful help to re-establish balance is to listen to inspired musical pieces. Works of quality elevate the capacity to reorganize the energies of the person and can be healing, as well as good reading material.

These suggestions are preliminary for living with inner peace and with wisdom in present times. When a person adopts them with determination, they can channel and radiate the energies towards the future in a world that currently is disorientated.

Finally, faith, self-discipline and the absence of mental speculations lead to contact with the inner life, a reunion that should not be delayed in these times that we are passing through.

Extracted from Bulletin Sinais, No 1, January-March 1999

About Trigueirinho and His Work

José Trigueirinho Netto (1931-2108) was born in Sao Paulo, Brazil. He lived in Europe for a number of years, where he maintained contact with individu-als who were advanced on the spiritual path, in-cluding Paul Brunton.

In his own life he was an example of the teachings that he transmitted through books and talks about the transcendence and elevation of the human being, the contact with the soul and with even more profound nuclei of the being, impersonal service, and the link with the Spiritual Hierarchies.

One of the fundamental elements of his work is to stimulate the expansion of human consciousness and to liberate it from the bonds that keep it imprisoned to material aspects of existence, both external and internal.

He was the founder of the Figueira Community of Light *(https://www.fraterinternacional.org/en/life-in-the-light-communities/* and one of the members of the Board of Directors of the Fraternity International Humanitarian Federation *(https://www.fraterinternacional.org/)* and co-founder of the Grace Mercy Order (http://www.gracemercyorder.org/). He also was an active collaborator, instructor and spiritual protector of three other communities located in Uruguay, Ar-gentina and Portugal.

In his last 30 years he lived in Figueira, in the interior of Minas Gerais, Brazil, a community that at present has approximately 300 residents and which is visited by thousands of collaborators who are members of a network of humanitarian services and of spiritual studies, which was was always followed closely by Trigueirinho.

Thanks to his inestimable instruction and his love for the Kingdoms of Nature, and as a result of the exemplary work that he himself implanted in the Figueira community, the Animal, Vegetable and Mineral Kingdoms are the recipients of loving treat-ment there.

Trigueirinho wrote 81 books published originally in Portuguese with many of them translated into Spanish, English, French and German. He gave more than 3,000 talks that were recorded live and which are available in CD, with some available in DVD and pen drive.

The primary focus of the first phase of Trigueirinho's work was concerned with self- knowledge, prayer, instruction and spiritual transformation. Following this, he began to transmit information with respect to Universal Life and about the assistance that humanity has from the beginning received by means of the Intra-terrestrial White Brotherhood which inhabits the Retreats and the Planetary Centers and also through the Cosmic Brotherhood of the Universe. He also mentions the presence of the Spiritual Hierarchy on the planet and the advent of the new humanity.

His work also includes themes relating to: the need for humanity to balance the negative karma that it has created in relation to the Kingdoms of Nature; the negative karmic burden that we carry from the history of slavery and the genocide of indigenous peoples; and the nature of spiritual work in groups. He also addresses issues of healing, a larger vision of astrology, the esoteric nature of symbols, sound and colors, and the divine feminine.

In his last eight years he analyzed with clarity, and with the wisdom that always characterized him, the messages that the Divinity has been giving to the planet as a warning to humanity (available from www.mensajerosdivinos.org/en).

His work reveals a real comprehension of the significance of all the Kingdoms of Nature on our planet, the true spiritual task of the human being, its place in the universe and also its responsibility before Creation.

Finally, he clarifies the reasons for the crisis that today is devastating humanity, teaching us how to avoid reacting negatively to an immanent natural catastrophe by contacting more subtle levels of consciousness, and opening perspectives for the beginning of a more luminous cycle for our race.

Books by Trigueirinho

(Books available in English have English title first)

Originally Published by Editora Pensamento Sao Paulo Brazil

1987

OUR LIFE IN DREAMS
NOSSA VIDA NOS SONHOS

A ENERGI A DOS RAIOS EM NOSSA VIDA
THE ENERGY OF THE RAYS IN OUR LIVES

1988

DO IRREAL AO REAL
FROM THE UNREAL TO THE REAL

Hora de Crescer Interiormente –

O Mito de Hércules Hoje
TIME FOR INNER GROWTH—
THE MYTH OF HERCULES TODAY

A Morte Sem Medo e Sem Culpa
DEATH WITHOUT FEAR OR GUILT

Caminhos Para A Cura Interior
WAYS TO INNER HEALING

1989

Erks – Mundo Interno
ERKS—THE INNER WORLD

Miz Tli Tlan – Um Mundo Que Desperta
MIZ TLI TLAN—AN AWAKENING WORLD

Aurora – Essência Cósmica Curadora
AURORA—COSMIC ESSENCE OF HEALING

Signs Of Contact
SINAIS DE CONTATO

O Novo Começo Do Mundo
THE NEW BEGINNING OF THE WORLD

A Quinta Raça
THE FIFTH RACE

Padrões de Conduta para a nova Humanidade
PATTERNS OF CONDUCT FOR THE NEW HUMANITY

Novos Sinais De Contato
NEW SIGNS OF CONTACT

Os Jardineiros Do Espaço
THE SPACE GARDENERS

1990

A Busca da Síntese
THE SEARCH FOR SYNTHESIS

Noah's Vessel
A NAVE DE NOÉ

Tempo de Retiro e Tempo de Vigília
A TIME OF RETREAT AND A TIME OF VIGIL

1991

Portas do Cosmos
GATEWAYS OF THE COSMOS

Encontro Interno – *A Consciência-Nave*
INNER ENCOUNTER – *The Consciousness Space Vessel*

A Hora do Resgate
  THE TIME OF RESCUE

O Livro dos Sinais
  THE BOOK OF SIGNS

Mirna Jad – *Santuário Interior*
  MIRNA JAD – *Inner Sanctuary*

As Chaves de Ouro
  THE GOLDEN KEYS

1992

Das Lutas à Paz
  FROM STRUGGLE TO PEACE

A Morada dos Elisíos
  THE ELYSIAN DWELLING PLACE

Hora de Curar – *A Existência Oculta*
  TIME FOR HEALING – *The Occult Existence*

O Ressurgimento de Fátima Lis
  THE RESURGENCE OF FATIMA LIS

História Escrita nos Espelhos
  Princípios de Comunicação Cósmic
  HISTORY WRITTEN IN THE MIRRORS -
  Principles of Cosmic Communication

Passos Atuais
  STEPS FOR NOW

Viagem por Mundos Sutis

TRAVEL THROUGH SUBTLE WORLDS

Segredos Desvelados – *Iberah e Anu Tea*
UNVEILED SECRETS – *Iberah and Anu Tea*

A Criação – *Nos Caminhos da Energia*
CREATION – *On the Paths of Energy*

The Mystery of the Cross In the Present Planetary Transition
O MISTÉRIO DA CRUZ NA ATUAL TRANSIÇÃO PLANETÁRIA

O Nascimento da Humanidade Futura
THE BIRTH OF THE FUTURE HUMANITY

1993

Aos Que Despertam
TO THOSE WHO AWAKEN

Paz Interna em Tempos Críticos
INNER PEACE IN CRITICAL TIMES

A Formação de Curadores
THE FORMATION OF HEALERS

Profecias aos Que Não Temem Dizer Sim
PROPHECIES FOR THOSE WHO ARE NOT AFRAID TO SAY YES

The Voice of Amhaj
A VOZ DE AMHAJ

O Visitante – **O Caminho Para Anu Tea**

THE VISITOR — *The Way to Anu Tea*

A Cura da Humanidade
THE HEALING OF HUMANITY

Os Números e a Vidas – *Uma Nova Compreensão da Simbologia Oculta nos Números*
NUMBERS AND LIFE — *A New Understanding of Occult Symbolism in Numbers*

Niskalkat – *Uma Mensagem para os Tempos de Emergência*
NISKALKAT — *A Message for Times of Emergency*

Encontros Com a Paz
ENCOUNTERS WITH PEACE

Novos Oráculos
NEW ORACLES

Um Novo Impulso Astrológico
A NEW ASTROLOGICAL IMPULSE

1994

Bases do Mundo Ardente – *Indicações para Contato com os Mundos suprafísicos*
BASES OF THE FIERY WORLD — *Indications for Contacts with Supraphysical Worlds*

Contatos com um Monastério Interaterreno
CONTACTS WITH AN INTRATERRESTRIAL MONASTERY

Os oceanos têm Ouvidos
 OCEANS HAVE EARS

A Trajetõria do Fogo
 THE PATH OF FIRE

Glossário Esotérico
 ESOTERIC LEXICON

1995

The Light Within You
 A LUZ DENTRO DE TI

1996

Doorway to a Kingdom PORTAL PARA UM REINO

Beyond Karma
 ALÉM DO CARMA

1997

We Are Not Alone
 NÃO ESTAMOS SÓS

Winds of the spirit
 VENTOS DO ESPÍRITO

Finding the Temple
 O ENCONTRO DO TEMPLO

There is Peace
 A PAZ EXISTE

1998

PATH WITHOUT SHADOWS

CAMINHO SEM SOMBRAS

MENSAGENS PARA UMA VIDA DE HARMONIA

MESSAGES FOR A LIFE OF HARMONY

1999

TOQUE DIVINO

THE DIVINE TOUCH

COLEÇÀO PEDAÇOS DE CÉU

BITS FROM HEAVEN COLLECTION

- **AROMAS DO ESPAÇO**
  AROMAS FROM SPACE
- **NOVA VIDA BATE À PORTA**
  A NEW LIFE AWAITS YOU
- **MAIS LUZ NO HORIZONTE**
  MORE LIGHT ON THE HORIZON
- **O CAMPANÁRIO CÓSMICO**
  THE COSMIC CAMPANILE
- **NADA NOS FALTA**
  WE LACK NOTHING
- **SAGRADOS MISTÉRIOS**
  SACRED MYSTERIES
- **ILHAS DE SALVAÇÁO**
  ISLANDS OF SALVATION

2002

CALLING HUMANITY
UM CHAMADO ESPECIAL

2004

ÉS VIAJANTE CÓSMICO
YOU ARE A COSMIC WAYFARER

IMPULSOS
IMPULSES

2005

PENSAMENTOS PARA TODO O ANO
THOUGHTS FOR THE WHOLE YEAR

2006

TRABALHO ESPIRITUAL COM A MENTE
SPIRITUAL WORK WITH THE MIND

2009

SIGNS OF BLAVATSKY — AN UNUSUAL ENCOUNTER FOR THE PRESENT TIME
SINAIS DE BLAVATSKY –
UM INUSITADO ENCONTRO NOS DIAS DE HOJE

Published by Editora Irdin
Carmo da Cachoeira, Minas Gerais, Brazil

2012

Consciências e Hierarquias
CONSCIOUSNESSES AND HIERARCHIES

2015

Mensagens Reunidas
COLLECTED MESSAGES

Mensagens para Sua Tranformaçã
MESSAGES FOR YOUR
TRANSFORMATION

2017

Páginas de Amor e Compreensão
PAGES OF LOVE AND COMPREHENSION

2018

Novos Tempos: Nova Postura
NEW TIMES: NEW ATTITUDE

2020

Versos Livres
OBRA PÓSTUMA

Trigueirinho's works are published by:

ASSOCIAÇÃO IRDIN EDITORA – www.irdin.org (selected titles of books in English and Portuguese and CDs in several languages), Carmo da Cachoeira, Brazil.

EDITORA PENSAMENTO – www.pensamento-cultrix.com.br (titles in Portuguese), São Paulo, Brazil.

EDITORIAL KIER – www.kier.com.ar (selected titles in Spanish), Buenos Aires, Argentina.

LICHTWELLE-VERLAG – www.lichtwelle-verlag.ch (selected titles in Spanish and German), Zurich, Switzerland.

SHASTI ASSOCIATION – www.shasti.org (selected titles in English), Mount Shasta, CA, USA.

Audios of Trigueirinho Lectures with Simultaneous English Translation

During over thirty years as Founder of the Figueira Community of Light, Trigueirinho gave bi-weekly lectures (called 'parthilha's or 'sharings') that were recorded live. Audience members were invited to submit questions to him which were placed in a small box and brought to him by an attendant. Arriving early, Trigueirinho sat at the lectern, reading through and taking notes on the audience questions. Thus, his lectures often began with the phrase "someone has asked a question...." After addressing some of these questions, he continued with the theme chosen for the day.

Approximately 70 of these 'sharings' were later dubbed with English translations. His voice or the translators can be augmented or diminished by adjusting the right-left balance of the recording.

To access these audio recordings go to the Shasti Association website:
www.shasti.org/instruction drop down the menu tab titled "Trigueirinho Instruction" and then click on "MP3 audios"

A Book to Be Written
A New Viewpoint of the Monad
Alopathic and Homeopathic Medicine
An Esoteric Dimension of Power
An Overview of Current Life
Angels and Humanity – 1
Angels and Humanity – 2
Angels and Humanity – 3
Angels and Humanity – 4
Bases of the Fiery World
Beyond Fire by Friction
Beyond Imperfection
Causal Body
Colors in Healing and the Formation of Our Light Vessel
Deep Healing
From the Human Kingdom to the Spiritual Kingdom
Getting through Today's Critical Times
Harmonization and Androgyny
How One Begins to Perceive One's Inner Self
How to Understand the Planetary Disasters
Human Trials | The Trials of the Soul
Information on the New Earth and the New Humanity
Inner and Outer Figueira
Instruction: a Step beyond Teaching
Liberating and Healing through Colors
Life in Cosmic Signs
New Supraterrestrial Pathways – 1
New Supraterrestrial Pathways – 2
New Supraterrestrial Pathways – 3
New Supraterrestrial Pathways – 4
Niskalkat

Noah's Vessel
On Vitality
Our Response to the Cosmos – 1
Our Response to the Cosmos – 2
Our Response to the Cosmos – 3
Our Response to the Cosmos – 4
Our Response to the Cosmos – 5
Our Response to the Cosmos – 6
Preparation for the Path of Initiation
Reflections on Illusion and Rescue
Reflections on Inner Attunement
Seeds of Inner Transformation
Seeking to Understand the Self
Several Levels of Spiritual Reading
Special Paths and the Path of the Majority
Spiritual Entities and Hierarchies
Spiritual Trials
Strengthening the Bases for the New Cycles
Subtle Bodies and Templing
Supraterrestrial Pathways – 1
Supraterrestrial Pathways – 2
Supraterrestrial Pathways – 3
Supraterrestrial Pathways – 4
Syntheses, Struggles and New Instructions
Taking Charge of One's Process of Dying – 1
Taking Charge of One's Process of Dying – 2
Taking Charge of One's Process of Dying – 3
The Art of Living in Current Times
The Cosmic Signs Reveal the Teaching – 1
The Cosmic Signs Reveal the Teaching – 2
The Desert
The Earth – Degeneration and Deliverance

The Era of the Gigantic Wave
The Importance of Self-Control in Epidemics and Other Risk Situations
The Light That Permeates Matter
The Mystery of the Cross in the Present Planetary Transition
The Doorways of the Planet – 1
The Doorways of the Planet – 2
The Doorways of the Planet – 3
The Doorways of the Planet – 4
The Doorways of the Planet – 5
The Days of Tomorrow
The Heart, the Ego and the Personality
The New Life That is Emerging
The Plan of Evolution and Us
The Practical Mystic
The Seventh Ray and the Devas
The Spark from the Divine Level
The Transmutation of the Logos of the Earth
The Voice of Amhaj
To Be Universal – Part 1
To Be Universal – Part 2
To Medical Doctors and Therapists
To Those Who Pray – 1
To Those Who Pray – 2
Towards Self Consecration
We are Part of the Cosmos
Working Spiritually with One's Mind
Working with the Feminine Polarity
Working with the Rays

www.ingramcontent.com/pod-product-compliance
Lightning Source LLC
Chambersburg PA
CBHW030328100526
44592CB00010B/617